OPTIONS TRADING

A BEGINNER'S GUIDE TO START INVESTING WITH A PRECISE STRATEGY AND ESTABLISHING A SOLID SOURCE OF INCOME FOR YOUR DAILY LIVING

Harvey D. McKinney

© **Copyright 2020 Harvey D. McKinney - All rights reserved.**

The content contained within this book may not be reproduced, duplicated or transmitted without direct written permission from the author or the publisher.
Under no circumstances will any blame or legal responsibility be held against the publisher, or author, for any damages, reparation, or monetary loss due to the information contained within this book. Either directly or indirectly.

Legal Notice:

This book is copyright protected. This book is only for personal use. You cannot amend, distribute, sell, use, quote or paraphrase any part, or the content within this book, without the consent of the author or publisher.

Disclaimer Notice:

Please note the information contained within this document is for educational and entertainment purposes only. All effort has been executed to present accurate, up to date, and reliable, complete information. No warranties of any kind are declared or implied. Readers acknowledge that the author is not engaging in the rendering of legal, financial, medical or professional advice. The content within this book has been derived from various sources. Please consult a licensed professional before attempting any techniques outlined in this book.
By reading this document, the reader agrees that under no circumstances is the author responsible for any losses, direct or indirect, which are incurred as a result of the use of information contained within this document, including, but not limited to, — errors, omissions, or inaccuracies.

Contents

Introduction 7

Introduction To Options 11

The Advantages of the Options 23

Trader's Mindset 31

Money Management 45

Risk Management 57

Building A Portfolio 69

Day Trading 81

Beginners Common Mistakes 97

How to Start Options Trading 107

Options Strategies 121

Understanding Passive Income 131

How Options Prices are Determined 141

Conclusion 153

Introduction

Option contracts usually refer to the purchase or sale of certain assets.

An option is a contract between two parties (a buyer and a seller), in which whoever buys the option acquires the right to exercise what the agreement indicates, although he will not have an obligation to do so.

Option contracts commonly refer to the purchase or sale of certain assets, which may be stocks, stock indices, bonds, or others. These contracts also establish that the operation must be carried out on a pre-established date (in the case of the European ones, since those of the US are exercised at any time) and at a fixed price at the time the contract is signed.

To purchase an option to buy or sell it is necessary to make an initial disbursement (called "premium"), whose value depends, fundamentally, on the price that the asset, that is the object of the contract, has on the market, on the variability of that price and of the period of time between the date on which the contract is signed and the date on which it expires.

Call and Put

The options that grant the right to buy are called 'Call', and those that allow the right to sell are called 'Put'. Additionally, it is called European options that can only be exercised on the date of exercise and American options that can be used at any time during the life of the contract.

When the time comes for the buying party to exercise the option, if it does, two situations occur:

Whoever appears as the seller of the option will be obliged to do what the said contract indicates; that is, sell or buy the asset to the counterparty, in case it decides to exercise its right to buy or sell.

Who appears as the option buyer will have the right to buy or sell the asset. However, if it does not suit you, you can refrain from making the transaction.

An option contract usually contains the following specifications:

- Exercise date: the expiration date of the right included in the option.
- Exercise price: agreed price for the purchase/sale of the asset referred to in the contract (called underlying asset).
- Option premium or price: amount paid to the counterparty to acquire the right to buy or sell.

- Rights acquired with the purchase of an option: they can be Call (right of purchase) and Put (right of sale).

- Types of Option: there may be Europeans, which are only exercised on the date of exercise or American, to be used at any time during the contract. There are, besides, other more complex types of options, the so-called "Exotic Options."

In international financial markets, the types of options that are traded on organized exchanges are typically American and European. In Chile, as with futures, there is no stock market for options.

Practical example

Purchase of a call option by an importing company to secure the Euro price on that day.

To better understand the use of options, this example is presented by an importing company that wants to ensure against increases in the price of the Euro.

To do so, you can buy a European call option today that gives you the right to buy a million euros, within three months, at $ 550 per euro. To acquire that right, the company pays $ 2 per euro, that is, the option premium has a cost of $ 2,000,000.

If on the expiration date of the option, the price of the euro in the market is over $ 550 (for example, at $ 560), the company will exercise the option to buy them, as it will only pay $ 550 per euro.

On the contrary, if on that date the market price of the Euro was below $ 550 (for example at $ 530), the company will not exercise the option, since it makes no sense to pay $ 550 per euro when it can be purchased at the market at $ 530; In this case, the option expires without being exercised.

The cash flows are as follows:

Today (April 10, 20XX).

Buy a European call option, which gives you the right to buy USD 1,000,000 to $ 550 on October 10, 20XX, as the value of the premium is 2 and 1,000,000 contracts are purchased (which means that the notional of the agreement is the US $ 1) there is a cash outlay of $ 2,000,000 for that concept.

Expiration date (October 30, 20XX)

If the Euro is above the exercise price of the option, it would be exercised, and $ 550 per euro will be paid, that is, $ 550,000,000.

Otherwise, the option expires if it is used, and the euros are acquired in the market.

The euros purchased are used to cancel the importation of goods or services.

INTRODUCTION TO OPTIONS

An option is basically an agreement on the underlying shares of stock. It's an agreement to exchange shares at a fixed price over a certain timeframe (they can be bought or sold). The first thing that you should understand about options is the following. Why would someone get involved with the options trading in the first place? Most people come to options trading with the hope of earning profits from trading the options themselves. And that's probably going to describe most readers of this book. But to truly understand what you're doing, you need to understand why options exist, to begin with.

There are probably three main reasons that options on stocks exist. The first reason is that it allows people that have shares of stock to earn money from their investment in the form of regular income. So, it can be an alternative to dividend income or even enhance dividend income. As we are going to see you later, if you own a minimum of 100 shares of some stock, this is a possibility. Then you can sell options against the stock and earn income from that over time intervals lasting from a week to a month. Obviously, such a move entails some risk, but people will enter positions of that type when the relative risk is low.

The second reason that people get involved with options is that they offer insurance against a collapse of the stock. So, once again, an option involves being able to trade shares of the stock at a fixed price that is set at the time the contract is originated. One type of contract allows the buyer to purchase shares, the other allows the buyer to sell shares. This allows people who own large numbers of shares to purchase something that provides protection of their investment that would allow them to sell the shares at a fixed price, in the event that their stock was declining by huge amounts on the market. So, the concept is exactly like paying insurance premiums. It's unclear how many people actually use this in practice, but this is one of the reasons that options exist. The way this would work would be that you pay someone a premium to secure the right to sell them your stock at a fixed price over some time frame. Then if the share price drops well below that degree to price, you would still be able to sell your shares and avoid huge losses that were occurring on the market.

The third reason that I would give for the existence of options is that it provides a way for people to make arrangements to purchase shares of stock at the prices that they find attractive, which aren't necessarily available on the market. So, there is a degree of speculation here. But let's just say that a particular stock you are interested in is trading at $100 a share. Furthermore, let's assume that people are extremely bullish on the stock and they are expecting it to rise by a great deal in the coming weeks. Maybe, it's earnings season.

During earnings season, stock can move by huge amounts. But before the earnings call, nobody knows whether the stock is going to go up or down or by how much it's going to move. An options contract could allow someone to speculate and set up a situation where they could profit from a huge move upward without having to actually invest in the stock.

So in that situation, if the stock declined instead, they wouldn't be out of much money. Just for an example, let's say they buy an options contract that allows them to purchase the shares (of the stock currently at $100) for $102, and the option costs two dollars per share. So, the stock would have to go to $104 or higher to make it worth it.

Typically, options contracts involve 100 shares. So, if the speculator bets wrong, the most they would be out would be $200.

Let's just say, after the earnings call, the share price jumps to $120. The speculator can exercise the option, which means they buy the shares at $102 per share. Then they can sell the stock on the market at the price of $120 per share. Taking into account the investment to buy the options contract, that basically leaves them with the sixteen $16 dollars per-share profit. Now, you might say well why didn't they just buy the shares that $100 a share? The reason is if they did that, they would actually be exposed to the stock to the fullest extent possible. Like we said, earnings calls can go both ways. Just recently, Netflix announced that they lost subscribers. In after-hours trading alone, the stock lost $43 per share. So, in our little example, we could say that the stock dropped instead of gaining, let's say to $80 per share. In that case, our speculator would've been in a major point of pain had they actually purchase the shares ahead of time. By doing the option instead, they set themselves up for profit while only risking a $200 loss. And it turns out that there are strategies you can use with options to profit no matter which way the stock moves. So, I didn't want to get too far ahead of ourselves, but an experienced options trader would have set up a trade designed to earn profits either way.

Types of Options

Options agreements come in two varieties. The first type of options contract is known as a call. A call option gives the buyer the possibility to buy some shares of stock at a fixed price. Usually, it's 100 shares. The agreed-upon value used to trade the shares is called the strike price. Every option comes with an expiration date, and so, if the buyer decides to purchase the shares, they must do so before the option expires. If the buyer decides to buy the shares, they are said to "exercise" the option. The party that sold to open the option, in that case, is said to be "assigned" if someone exercises the contract.

Options can be classified by the way they can be exercised. The possibilities are American-style or European-style. If you can exercise the option on any date, it's known as American style.

If the contract is a European style, the option can only be exercised on the day it expires. It's important to note that these terms don't necessarily mean that the option is trading in Europe or America. Although most options in America are American-style, there are some that are European style. Two examples are SPX and RUT. These are options used to follow the S & P 500 index and the Russell 2000 index. But the vast majority of options you're going to come across are going to be American style. If you sell options, this is something you need to be aware of. That means at any time that the option is an open position for you as a seller, you could be assigned.

The basic rule for a call option is that this is a bullish purchase. If you invest in a call option, your expectation is that's the price of the shares is going to rise. There are two ways that you can take advantage of this. The first way is to simply trade the option. As we will see later, small moves in the stock price translate into big moves for options prices. So, if the stock goes up in price, you can sell the option and make a profit.

The second way to profit would be to actually exercise the right to buy the shares. In that situation, you would buy the shares for the price per share given by the strike and then sell them on the open market to make a profit. In order to make money, the price on the market must rise to a level greater than the strike price added to the amount you paid to buy in the position.

So, if you purchased a $50 option for $1, meaning the strike price is $50, the price on the market would have to rise to $51 or higher to make exercising the option profitable.

The rule is that call options increase in price or value primarily when stock prices are rising. But, as we'll see, options are impacted by some other factors as well. But the general bet with a call option is earning profits when the underlying stock goes up in value.

Before we move on to consider the other major class of options, we need to make a clear distinction between selling and buying options. We can loosely use this language, but, actually, be applying it in very different contexts. First, let's consider simple options trading which is what most readers are going to be interested in. In this case, you enter a position by purchasing an option. So in market jargon, we would say that you are buying to open. So, in other words, you open your position by purchasing an option. If you buy to open an option you are never at risk of being assigned the shares of stock. So, you can sell the option and that carries no risk to you whatsoever. The only risk that you would face would be having to sell the option for a discount compared to what you paid to enter the position.

In contrast, you can also sell to open an options position. When you do that, you are at risk for the assignment with regard to the shares of stock. So that doesn't entail some risk but there are many reasons that people would choose to sell to open an options position. Also, you can sell to open positions in order to earn income from the premium.

The second type of option is called a put. A put option is a contract that allows the buyer to sell shares to the writer of the contract. This would be 100 of stock with a price given by the strike price. So, a put option has a strike price and expiration date just like a call option.

Put options actually increase in value if the market price of the stock declines. So if you buy a put, you are basically shorting the stock. If you intend to exercise the option, it would work in the following way. To use specific numbers, consider an example with the strike price of the option at $100 dollars per share. Then we will suppose that the company had a negative earnings call and the share price drop to $70 a share overnight. If you held the put option, you could buy the shares on the market at $70 a share. Then you can "exercise the option". That means you would sell the shares at the price of $100 a share because that was the strike price on the contract. So, you would make nearly a $30 profit per share by engaging in this trade. The profit would be given by the strike price minus the premium paid to buy the option minus the price you purchase the shares for on the market. So if we just imagine that the option cost $2 a share, the profit, in this case, would be $100 - $2 -$70 = $28 per share. Since there are 100 shares per option contract, that would mean a profit of $2800.

The general rule for put options, as we said, is that they increase in value when the share price drops. So many options traders are not looking to actually exercise the option. What they want to do is still hold the put option if there is a belief that the share price will decline, and then trade the put option on the market at a profit if the share price actually drops.

So, you might ask why would someone sell to open a put option? People sell put options in order to make money from the premiums. This can be done alone or in conjunction with a special option strategy that may involve both types of options. If you sell a put option, obviously you're hoping that the share price is not going to drop far enough to make it worth it to exercise. And in most circumstances, that's actually going to be the case. A higher risk here would be selling to open a put with a strike price that is near current market prices.

Some Industry Jargon

Okay, so let's get some jargon out of the way so that you can navigate the options markets and understand what people are talking about. We have already mentioned a few of the terms, but let's review them right now.

Strike Price

If an option is actually exercised, shares are traded at the strike price. So, this is the price per share that the shares of stock would be sold to a buyer if we are talking about a call option. If instead, it's a put option, this is the price per share that the trader who sold to open the contract agrees to pay in order to purchase the shares from the buyer of an option. The strike price is set when the contract is opened and is good until the option expires.

Expiration Date

Every option comes with an expiration date. When trading options, it's important to know when the expiration date is. If you are only trading options with no intent to exercise them, you don't want to ever be stuck with an option on the expiration day. Options typically expire on Fridays, but for heavily traded options on exchange-traded funds, they expire Monday, Wednesday, and Friday. A "standard" option is one that lasts a month. These options will expire on a Friday. It will be the third week of the month, but there are options that only last for one week (called "weeklies") and there are also options that last several weeks to two years. An option that lasts for more than a year is called "LEAPS" which means Long-term Equity Appreciation Security. There is nothing special about them other than the expiration date, otherwise, they are just like other options.

Time Decay

Since something that expires has less value the less time there is available on the contract, options suffer from a problem called "time decay". Options get some of the pricing from "extrinsic" or "time" value. The smaller the amount of time remaining on the contract, the lower the time value. If the stock is moving in a favorable direction, however, the value of the option that is related to the current market cost of the stock and a couple of other factors can overwhelm time decay.

To know what the time decay is, you can look up a quantity called theta that will be listed for every option. It will tell you how much the option price is going to drop at the market open the following day. So, if an option has a theta of -0.11, that means that it's going to drop in price by 100 shares x $0.11 = $11 at the next market open. This may or may not be important. Other factors can swamp that $11 and make it irrelevant. But you need to be aware of it.

In the Money

If the strike price favorably positioned with respect to current market prices, it is known by this term. For a call option, it will be in the money if the share price (on the market) of the stock is greater than the price known as the strike price. For a put option, it will be in the money if the price that would be paid for the stock just buying it is less than the strike price. When an option is in the money, its value has heavily influenced the price that the stock is trading at. In the ideal situation, which can happen as an in the money call option approaches expiration, a $1 increase in the stock price will translate into a $100 change in the price of the option that would go up as well. Of course, this cuts both ways, so it can mean a $100 loss if the share price is moving the other way.

The Advantages of the Options

Limit Your Risk

A good reason to go with buying options is that you will be able to limit your risk down to just the amount of money that you pay for the premium. With other investment options, you could end up losing a lot of money, even money that you did not invest to begin with, but this does not happen when you are working with options.

Let's say that you saw that the prices of cows were about to go up. You could pay some money upfront and enter into a contract with someone else to sell your five cows for $2000. At this point, since you are working with an options contract, you did not buy the cows upfront.

On the other hand, if you had gone up to the other person and purchased those cows straight up for a cost of $10,000, you could end up in trouble. For this example, the price of the cows may end up falling by $500, rather than going up by $500, and you would end up losing $2500 in the process. Since you went into the options contract though, you would stand to lose no more than $250 if the prices were to fall afterward. You still stand to lose some money, but it is a lot less than you would have lost otherwise.

Better Leverage for the Money

You will find that when you are working with options, it can provide you with some good leveraging power. A trader will be able to buy an option position that will imitate their stock position quite a bit, but it will end up saving them a lot of money in the process.

Let's say that you saw that there was an opportunity to make a profitable trade, you were only able to spare about $1000 to purchase the stock, but you didn't know that options were available. If we were still talking about the cows from before, you would not be able to purchase even one cow for the money (remember that they are about $2000 each without the options contract), and so you would completely miss out on the possibility to make a profit.

But, if you decided to purchase with an options contract, rather than purchasing the underlying asset outright, the dynamics have completely changed. This could result in an investment of just $250 to get started. The premium on the options contract is a fraction of the total cost, allowing you to get in on the trade for a lot less money. If you look into options contracts, you will be able to make more purchases, and potentially more money, compared to some of the other stock choices you can make.

Higher Percentage of Returns

As mentioned, an options trader is only going to pay a fraction of the value of the asset just to have some control over that asset. This will allow the trader to earn more money than what they would be able to earn when they purchase the asset upfront and then try to sell it. Let's take a look at an example of how this can work.

Going back to the idea of the cows, the market price at the beginning of this trade is $2000. For a regular cattle trader, one who doesn't know anything about options, had the $2000 in hand and believed that the price of the cattle is going to go up, he would only have the opportunity to purchase on cow. If the price of the cows goes up to $2500, this trader will only be able to make a profit of $500. This isn't bad, but since there is a big risk with this option, it is not always the best.

On the other hand, a trader who knows a bit about options will be able to do things a bit different. If you had $2000, you could choose to purchase eight options contracts, with a premium of $50. This means that you now have the purchasing rights for a total of 40 cows rather than the 1 cow the other trader had.

With the same profit of $500 per cow, your profit would be $18,000 (this includes the $500 per cow minus the $2000 you spent in the beginning to purchase the contracts). You earned thousands of dollars more compared to the original trader, but you used the same amount of money to get started.

Helps to Hedge Intraday or Futures Trades

It is common for traders to purchase or short-sell Futures contracts because they expect them to move in one direction or another. Intraday traders may do the same thing, because they will purchase a large number of shares in the hopes that they are going to move down or up during that day. If the trader ends up picking the wrong direction on the Futures or the intraday trades, they may end up losing a lot of weight. Unless you put in a stop-loss, it is possible for you to lose an unlimited amount of money in the process.

You may not be complaining when this goes the right way and you earn unlimited profits, but if you go with one of these trades and you don't hedge your position, you are going to complain when you start losing a lot of money. If you have an understanding on how trading options works, you could buy call or put options to help ensure that you are not going to end up with an unlimited loss. The right options choice is going to help control your loss the moment that the intraday or futures positions starts going against what you wanted.

While there are a lot of great investment choices that you can make, none of them are going to limit your risk as much as options while still providing you with a great potential to make money in the process. This is a great investment for anyone, whether they are just getting started with investing or they have been in the market for a long time.

Flexibility and versatility

The investment strategy of buying stocks doesn't confer to investors avenues of risk limitation or strategies of increasing their earning potential. As a stock trader, the method of earning a profit is linear, i.e., you either buy stocks that you think will appreciate or short sell stocks that you think will depreciate. But when it comes to options trading, the flexibility and versatility afford an investor many opportunities of earning huge profits as dictated by the prevailing markets. Options can be purchased or sold based on a wide selection of underlying assets. You can speculate on the movement of stock price, commodities, foreign currencies, indices, etc. The challenge is to identify opportunities for profitable trades. Spreads can make your trades more flexible, and they can be applied in hedging positions as well, which is a critical step during uncertain market conditions. A trader can also profit from stagnant markets by utilizing options spreads, an action that is hard to replicate in stock trading.

Helps to Hedge Intraday or Futures Trades

It is common for traders to purchase or short-sell Futures contracts because they expect them to move in one direction or another. Intraday traders may do the same thing because they will purchase a large number of shares in the hopes that they are going to move down or up during that day. If the trader ends up picking the wrong direction on the Futures or the intraday trades, they may end up losing a lot of weight. Unless you put in a stop-loss, it is possible for you to lose an unlimited amount of money in the process.

You may not be complaining when this goes the right way and you earn unlimited profits, but if you go with one of these trades and you don't hedge your position, you are going to complain when you start losing a lot of money. If you have an understanding of how trading options works, you could buy call or put options to help ensure that you are not going to end up with an unlimited loss. The right options choice is going to help control your loss the moment that the intraday or futures positions start going against what you wanted.

Though there exist several great investment choices that you can make, none of them are going to limit your risk as much as options while still providing you with a great potential to make money in the process. This is a great investment for anyone, whether they are just getting started with investing or they have been in the market for a long time.

Can Options Work for You?

Even after you understand the benefits that the options offer, you may be wondering if you have what it takes to trade them profitably. That depends more on commitment than any sort of innate ability.

Almost anyone can learn to trade options successfully. You don't have to be a financial whiz or a stock market expert. The only math that's required is eighth-grade arithmetic. But you will need some discipline, and a good understanding of the basic concepts I present in this book.

Once you get a handle on the fundamentals, you have a lot of choices about how to use options. Some strategies require a fair amount of skill and close attention to price movements. Others have a high probability of success and don't require a lot of time or attention.

When you're ready to start trading, it's important to get your feet wet by making simulated trades in a paper trading account where you aren't risking real money. Then you can take the next step by trading in a live account and taking very small positions to limit your risk.

From that point on, you can develop your options trading skills at your own pace and choose the strategies and level of risk that best suit you. The possibilities are almost endless.

Trader's Mindset

Trading psychology is the mental state and emotions that determine the success or failure of trading options. It represents the aspect of your behavior that dictates the decisions you make when faced with a trade. The psychology is vital to any trade and can be compared to experience, knowledge, and skills in determining your success as a trader.

When you decide to start options trading, you need to grasp the concept of risk-taking and discipline that determines the implementation of any trade.

The two most common emotions are greed and fear, while others are regret and hope.

Fear

At any given time, fear represents one of the worst kinds of emotions that you can have. Check in your newspaper one day, and you read about a steep selloff, and the next thing is trying to rack your brain about what to do next even if it isn't the right action at that time.

Many investors think that they know what will happen in the next few days, which makes them have a lot of confidence in the outcome of the trade. This leads to investors getting into the trade at a level that is too high or too low, which in turn makes them react emotionally.

As the trader puts a lot of hope on the single trade, the level of fear tends to increase, and hesitation and caution kick in.

Fear is part of every trader, but skilled traders have the capacity to manage the fear. There are various types of fears that you will experience, let us look at a few of them:

The Fear to Lose

Have you ever entered a trade and all you could think about is losing? The fear of losing makes it hard for you to execute the perfect strategy or enter or exit a strategy at the right time.

As a trader, you know that you need to make timely decisions when the strategy signals you to take one. When you have fear guiding you, the level of confidence drops, and you don't have the ability to execute the strategy the right way, at the right time. When a strategy fails, you lose trust in your abilities as well as strategy.

When you lose trust in many of the strategies, you end up with analysis paralysis, whereby you don't have the capacity to pull the trigger on any decision that you make. Making a move becomes a huge challenge.

When you cannot pull the trigger, all you can think about is staying away from the pain of losing, while you need to move towards gains.

No trader likes to lose, but it is a fact that even the best traders will make losses once in a while. The key is for them to make more profitable trades that allow them to stay in the game.

When you worry too much, you end up being distracted from your execution process, and instead, you focus on the results.

To reduce the fear in trading, you need to accept losses. The probability of losing or making a profit is 50/50, and you need to accept this fact and accept a trade, whether it is a sell or a buy signal.

The Fear of a Positive Trend Going Negative (and Vice Versa)

Many traders choose to go for quick profits and then leave the losses to run down. Many traders want to convince themselves that they have made some money for the day, so they tend to go for a quick profit so that they have the winning feeling.

So, what should you do instead? You need to stick with the trend. When you notice a trend is starting, it is good to stay with the trend until you have a signal that the trend is about to reverse. It is only then that you exit this position.

To understand this concept, you need to consider the history of the market. History is good at pointing out that times change, and trends can go either way. Remember that no one knows the exact time the trend will start or end; all you need to do is wait upon the signal.

The Fear of Missing Out

For every trade, you have people that doubt the capacity of the trade to go through. After you place the trade, you will be faced with many skeptics that will doubt the whole procedure and leave you wondering whether to exit the strategy or not.

This fear is also characterized by greed – because you aren't working on the premise of making a successful trade rather the fact that the security is rising without you having a piece of the pie.

This fear is usually based on information that there is a trend which you missed that you would have capitalized on.

This fear has a downside – you will forget about any potential risk associated with the trade and instead think that you have the capacity to make a profit because other people benefited from the action.

Fear of Being Wrong

Many traders put too much emphasis on being right that they forget that this is a business they should run the right way. They also forget that being successful is all about knowing the trend and how it affects their engagement.

When you follow the best timing strategy, you create many positive results over a certain time.

The uncanny desire to focus on always being right instead of focusing on making money is a great part of your ego, and to stay on the right path; you need to trade without your ego for once.

If you accommodate a perfectionist mentality when you get into trades, you will be after failure because you will experience a lot of losses as well. Perfectionists don't take losses the right way, and this translates into fear.

Ways to Overcome Fear in Trading

As you can see, it is obvious that fear can lead to losses. So, how can you avoid this fear and become successful?

- ✓ Learn

You need to find a way to get knowledge so that you have the basis for making decisions. When you know all there is to know about options, you know what to buy and when to sell, and learn which ones to watch. You are then more comfortable making the right decisions.

✓ Have Goals

What are your short term and long-term goals? Setting the right goals helps you to overcome fear. When you have goals, you have rules that dictate how you behave, even in times of fear. You also have a timeline for your journey.

✓ Envision the Bigger Picture

You always need to evaluate your choices at all times and see what you have gained or lost so far for taking some steps. Understanding the mistakes, you made gives you guidance to make better decisions in the future.

✓ Start Small

Many traders that subscribe to fear have lost a lot before. They put a lot of funds on the line and ended up losing, which in turn made them fear to place other trades. Begin with small sums so that you don't risk too much to put fear in you. Once you get more confident, you can invest larger sums so that you enjoy more profit.

- ✓ Use the Right Strategy

Having the right trading strategy makes it easy to execute your trades successfully. Make sure you look at various options trading strategies so that you know which one is ideal for your situation and skills.

Many strategies can help you succeed, but others might leave you confused. If you have a strategy that doesn't give you the returns you desire, then adjust it to suit your needs over time. Refine it till you are comfortable with its performance.

- ✓ Go Simple

When you have a strategy that is simple and straightforward, you will be less likely to lose confidence along the way because you know what to expect.

Additionally, the easier the strategy, the faster it will be to spot any issues.

- ✓ Don't Hesitate

At times you have to jump into the fray even if you aren't so comfortable with the way it works. Once you begin taking steps, you will learn more about the trade.

However, you always need to be prepared when taking any trade. The more prepared you are, the easier it will be for you to run successful trades.

✓ Don't Give Up

Things might not always go as you expect them to do. Remember that mistakes are there to give you lessons that will make you a better trader. When you lose, take time to identify the mistake you made and then correct it, then try again.

Greed

This refers to a selfish desire to get more money than you need from a trade. When the desire to get more than you can usually make takes over your decision-making process, you are looking at failure.

Greed is seen to be more detrimental than fear. Yes, fear can make you lose trades, but the good thing is that you get to preserve your capital. On the other hand, greed places you in a situation where you spend your capital faster than you return it. It pushes you to act when you shouldn't be acting at all.

The Danger of Being Greedy

When you are greedy, you end up acting irrationally. Irrational trading behavior can be overtrading, overleveraging, holding onto trades for too long, or chasing different markets.

The more greed you have, the more foolish you act. If you reach a point at which greed takes over from common sense, then you are overdoing it.

When you are greedy, you also end up risking way much more than you can handle and you end up with a loss. You also have unrealistic expectations from the market, which makes it seem as if you are after just money and nothing else.

When you are greedy, you also start trading prematurely without any knowledge of the options trading market.

When you are too greedy, your judgment is clouded, and you won't think about any negative consequences that might result when you make certain decisions.

Many traders that were too greedy ended up giving up after making this mistake in the initial trading phase.

How to Overcome Greed

Like any other endeavor in trading, you need a lot of effort to overcome greed. It might not be easy because we are talking about human emotions here, but it is possible.

First, you have to know that every call you make won't be the right one at all times. There are times when you won't make the right move, and you will end up losing money. At times you will miss the perfect strategy altogether, and you won't move a step ahead.

Secondly, you have to agree that the market is way bigger than you. When you do this, you will accept and make mistakes in the process.

Hope

Hope is what keeps a trading expectation alive when it has reached reversal. Hope is usually factored in the mind of a trader that has placed a huge amount on a trade. Many traders also go for hope when they wish to recoup past losses. These traders are always hopeful that the next trade will be the best, and they end up placing more than they should on the trade.

This type of emotion is dangerous because the market doesn't care at all about your hopes and will take your money.

Regret

This is the feeling of disappointment or sadness over a trade that has been done, especially when it has resulted in a loss.

Focusing too much on missing on trade makes the trader not to move forward. After you learn the lessons after such a loss, you need to understand the mistakes you made then move ahead.

When you decide to let regret to rule your thinking, you start chasing markets with the hopes that you will end up making money on a position by doubling the entrance price.

Things That Distinguish Winning and Losing Traders in Options Trading

<u>Handling Analysis Paralysis</u>

Traders usually start their journey getting the right knowledge. This knowledge comes in the form of books, coaches, and more. Once you have the information, the next step is to take it and use it in the market. The lucky ones will place various trades, and then things will go their way, while for others, the money will go down the drain.

Trading requires you to determine the right time to place a trade or exit one. The successful trader will know when to use a strategy, but the losing trader will end up placing trade after trade without any success at all.

Understanding the Nature of the Market

You need to understand that no market is constant – it changes with time. At times, the market will go along with your analysis, while at times; it might go the opposite direction.

Accept the Risk

No one wants to lose money on the markets. You need to come up with a strategy that allows you to know when to stop and reflect or tap out. At times you have to pull the plug regardless of how much you have invested in research and your expectations.

Know When to Take Profits

So, what determines the exit strategy? You need to know what point requires you to say this profit is enough for me. At times, it might be dictated by the changes in the trend or your rules of trading. Don't hold on to a trade for too long because it is always better to have some profit than wait and end up losing everything.

Understanding When you are Wrong

You need to remember that the options trading market is random, and you need to admit when you are wrong at times. This is because failure to admit will lead you to greed that might cloud your judgment.

When it comes to trading options, you have various traps that lead to fear or greed. Most of these traps come on expiration day; let us look at the various traps to avoid.

Money Management

Money management is how you handle your finances, your savings, your expenditure, and investments. It is making sure you can survive a financial crisis. It means planning a budget for your long-term goals and also making investments that will help you to successfully achieve your goals. When you manage your money, you will be able to make wise purchases. Otherwise, you will always complain of having less amount of money no matter how much your income is. It can also be known as investment management.

Money management is more about risk. When you have better money management skills, you will reduce the risk. You must understand all the areas of money management to be able to avoid any risks. Plan with a negative bias, always ask yourself "what-if" scenarios, take action, and plan. When budgeting for money management, make sure you are spending less than what you save. Excellent money management will help you monitor your spending before going beyond your budget. By doing this, you will secure your savings.

You will be able to invest if you make the right decisions. Avoiding taking on more risks will help you reach your financial goals.

The strategies you use in your investments play a significant role in your success. When you decide to invest, the first important thing to focus on is the risk involved, and you can avoid it. Here are some of the basics, advantages, and disadvantages of money management.

The Basics of Money Management

Money management is a wide term that involves solutions and services in the entire investment industry. You can now have a wide range of resources in today's market and also phone applications to help you manage all your finances. Investors can also seek services from a financial advisor for professional money management. Financial advisors work with private banking and even brokerage services to offer money management plans involving services like retirement and estate planning.

The Advantages of Money Management

1.Better tracking of your money. When you have a reasonable budgeting plan, you can track how you use your money, and you can monitor every expense. This is a significant benefit to you, as you can spend less and end up saving more money. Monitor your expenses for some months and then change your budgeting by removing the less required expense and allocate that money to your savings plan, a retirement plan, or a vacation fund. Excellent money management will help you stay on track; you will be able to pay your bills on time, will be able to stay within your limit, and avoid bank account overdraws. Poor money management can put you in bad debt quicker than a blink of an eye. You can prevent those nasty fees charges when you go over your limit. By having an excellent budgeting plan, you will avoid overspending.

2.A good retirement plan. Better money management and savings plans will help you in the long term. You will be able to secure your future and have an excellent retirement plan. With better money management skills will give you a better retirement plan for you. No matter how much you save, even when you save and invest a small amount of money, it will provide you with a more significant amount for your retirement later in life.

3.Peace of mind. Proper money management brings you peace of mind. Having bills on the counter and having no idea on how you will pay the bills or not having the money to purchase something that you needed. All these issues can be difficult to face each day. Managing your money wisely and experience all the benefits of sound money management, you will enjoy peace of mind, and you can provide for yourself and your family, too.

The Disadvantages of Money management

1.Rapid changes. With the rapid changes in the financial world, it is required to change your management plans every time. It is sometimes challenging to adjust your planning to incorporate the fast-changing situations. Unless your plan can help to adopt the new techniques, it will be limited.

2.Time-consuming. Managing your money can sometimes be a time-consuming exercise. It requires you to make the estimates as accurate as possible. However, you can use software and mobile applications to assist you with planning, and this may reduce the time you will take if you were not using the technologies. And if you have less knowledge about money management, it will take you more time to achieve this.

3.Inaccuracy. When planning, you make a lot of assumptions in terms of estimation of your expenses. Any shift like economic downturn or the change in the currency rate or interest rates can change your estimates in your planning.

What Are Money Skills?

People giving out money advice sometimes overcomplicates things. Some myths make it harder to save money and be rich, so try to forget about them. Also, some of the tips available are overwhelming and seem unnecessary. Most successful people can balance their check without a business degree or any financial training. However, you can get by with basic information about excellent money skills.

What are these money skills that everyone should know about? Don't try to memorize all the rules. Try to understand each one of them and implement them in your day-to-day life. I will list down some money skills that will set you up on a path to financial freedom.

Budget without "budgeting". Budgeting may seem like a basic thing, but it is arguably not. Only a few households keep a detailed budget.

This is critical behavior, mainly if you are not hitting your primary goals—for example, fully funding your emergency fund. Luckily, you can use tools like Excel sheets and other software that are tailor-made for different personalities and requirements. Is staying disciplined in your budgeting and spending a problem for you? Consider the envelope method. From the name, this method involves having physical envelopes for your expenses and keep your cash in. This method can help you to reset your mind's bad habits. Budgeting is a process, and once your savings start to grow, you can switch to auto-deposits.

Manage debt with clear eyes. Not all debts are equal. There is student debt, which you can pay off by the increase in your income. Getting a mortgage is cheaper than renting. Some of these debts can be an investment in the future; however, you still have to make a plan for tackling these debts.

There are two methods of paying off your debts, and both ways use snow metaphors. One of the methods is the avalanche approach, where you start with the highest-interest debts first. The other one is the snowball approach, where you start with the smallest and easiest debts to pay off first. The avalanche method is usually the best to choose in terms of saving. Let's say you have $43,000 of debts of car loans, student debt, and credit card debt. When you use the avalanche method, you will end up saving up to over $1,000 a month sooner on interest payments. However, the snowball method is also appealing. If small victories keep you going, then you can consider choosing this method. It all depends on your personality.

Have a written plan. Financial freedom is a choice. The financial decision you make today will determine how close or far you are moving from your financial goals. Write down a financial goals plan, and this plan will guide you throughout your journey to financial success. The written plan is not about writing down some motivation words through your plans. Instead, write more detailed information defining every aspect of your financial goals and include illustrations and exact words and figures. Define your timeline and quantum of your money management to achieve your financial goals.

Start right away. Start your savings earlier to be able to achieve your financial success and start planning your retirement. You don't have to be a financial guru to begin. With early savings, you will have enough time to grow your savings rate.

Don't touch your social security. Do not tap into your social security no matter what urgent your need is as social security should be the last option. Social security is to be used after your retirement, and this means you might meet your daily expenses with your social security amount. Your pension would be better if you wait longer before you claim your social security.

Plan your risks. The higher the risk, the higher your returns will be. However, this doesn't mean you should rush into a high-risk investment with thinking twice. Based on someone's financial status, each person can afford to take risks differently. So you need to evaluate your financial situation and if you can handle a loss financially. By doing this, you will have a clear image of the risk you can afford to handle.

Capital preservation should be your top priority when planning for your retirement. Access your risk profile before investing.

Plan your taxes. Between your income, expenditures, and savings, one compulsory factor is taxes. As a citizen of a country, you should be familiar with the taxation laws and how your income is taxed. Use your knowledge of tax planning and try to save more on your funds. Learning Tax planning will help you when you retire, you will be able to carefully handle your investments which are liable to be taxed.

Apply the 5% rule. This is a beneficial and practical rule. It merely means that you cut down on your expenses by 5% from your top 3 expenses in your categories yearly. To be able to apply this skill, you first have to list down your top 3 expenses in your categories, then break them down within the categories, and by doing this, you will know which areas you can save money on. For example, dining out is part of your monthly expenses, and this is essential to make it to your list. You can apply this skill by, for example, if your monthly expense on dining out is substantial and makes to the list, then find ways to reduce the costs by probably packing your lunch to take with you to the office or limit the dining out two times a month. You can quickly achieve your financial goals by breaking down into habits and creating good savings habits.

Why Is Money Management Important?

Money turns to wealth when it is well-managed. It is an instrument which is used to pursue wealth. For wealthy people, having and spending money does not bring them happiness, which gives them joy is having a steady income, and they can go on achieving their goals—and being able to leave a legacy to their loved ones. Money management focuses on your habits, and your decision making can have affected the outcome in your long-term strategies. In pursuit of wealth, there are many powerful elements such as debts, risks, and taxes that can take away all the hard work you have put in to achieve your goals. This is a life skill that everyone must learn. You don't have to be financially savvy to start managing your money. There is plenty of information available to help you better understand your finances. The following are the importance of money management:

- Establishing clear goals. Have a clear approach to your decision in money management to build your wealth.

Making the best decision will bring you closer to your goals. Also, set some clear and realistic goals which you want to achieve and set a time horizon for achieving them. Setting up clear goals will help you track where you are, and this will help you see your progress towards your goals. Some people give up earlier due to not being able to see their progress. You can be able to see your progress and stay encouraged if you break your goals into short term milestones. Finally, have clear and quantifiable goals to help you to make clear decisions. Abandon any choices that will not get you closer to your destination.

- Controlling your cash flow. Spend less than what you earn will help you accumulate wealth. You can't be financially successful if you are not tracking and monitoring your expenditure. Drawing up a spending plan and religiously following the plan might seem trivial, but it's central to the success of the wealthiest people in the world. If you own a business, your goal will be to find ways of increasing your monthly profits, which you will use to invest in for more growth. You will learn how to prioritize your spending when you have a solid money management plan and also by making the right decisions, which will bring you closer to your goals.

- Budgeting. Creating a household income budget is an essential part of personal money management. Budgeting will help you better understand your cash flow, thus giving you a clear understanding of your current financial situation.

- Debt management. There is proper financial education to help you understand consumer debt and how it works. There are also financial advisers and credit counselors who provide advice on how you can check your debts, your loan terms, and how you can pay off the debt quickly and stress-free.

- Managing your risks. Your risk exposure increases as you continue accumulating your wealth. You might think that wealth can make life easier, but it does not. The ignored reality is that it can make life more complicated. Getting a bigger house, expensive cars, and lavish lifestyles. These bring financial exposure and the potential to lose if all is great.

Have a risk management assessment in your money management plan with also protection strategies to help prepare you for the unexpected. Some of the unintended exposure include:

- Income loss due to illness or accident

- Death of the breadwinner in the family

- Asset exposure to liability claims

Money management will provide you with a 360-degree view of your financial status, and having financial discipline will assist you in overcoming these obstacles. With a solid money management principle, you will have better control of your financial goals.

Being tax efficient. Paying taxes is a responsibility; however, there is no obligation to paying more than necessary. Most people are not aware of how much taxes they are paying and the results of the unnecessary taxes and how it affects their wealth accumulation abilities. Money management does not focus on what you make but what you get after paying your taxes. Tax characteristics of your investment and your overall portfolio must be considered. The first thing to consider is the account location, the money allocation on different types of accounts based on respective tax treatment. Secondly, the asset location, wherein you allocate different types of investments among the different types of accounts on the tax treatment—for example, allocating your least tax-efficient assets to a tax-deferred account such as 401(k).

The taxable accounts can hold in a tax-efficient investment such as low turnover funds. This will give you more options for distribution of income in the more tax-efficient retirement, thus enabling you to accumulate more wealth faster.

Risk Management

Risk management has many different elements to both quantitative and qualitative. When it comes to options trading, the quantitative side is minimal thanks to the nature of options limiting risk by themselves. However, the qualitative side deserves a lot of attention.

Risk

So what is risk anyway? Logically, it is the probability of you losing all of your money. In trading terms, you can think of it as being the probability of your actions putting you on a path to losing all of your capital. A good way to think about the need for good risk management is to ask yourself what a bad trader would do? Forget trading, what would a bad business person do with their capital?

Well, they would spend it on useless stuff that adds nothing to the bottom line. They would also increase expenses, market poorly, not take care of their employees, and be indiscipline with regards to their processes. While trading, you don't have employees or marketing needs, so you don't need to worry about that.

Do you have suppliers and costs? Well, yes, you do. Your supplier is your broker, and you pay fees to execute your trades. That is the cost of access. In directional trading, you have high costs as well because taking losses is a necessary part of trading. With market neutral or non-directional trading, your losses are going to be minimal, but you should still seek to minimize them.

What about discipline? Do you think you can trade and analyze the market well if you've just returned home from your job and are tired? If you didn't sleep properly last night? Or if you've argued with your spouse or partner? The point I'm making is that the more you behave like a terrible business owner, the more you increase your risk of failure.

Odds and Averages

Trading requires you to think a bit differently about profitability. This is a natural product of linear or ordered thinking. The market, however, is chaotic and linear thinking is going to get you nowhere.

Instead, you need to think in terms of averages and odds. Averages imply that you need to worry about your average loss size and your average win size. Seek to decrease the former and increase the latter. Notice that when we talk about averages, we're not necessarily talking about reducing the total number of losses. You can reduce the average by either reducing the sum of your losses or by increasing the number of losing trades while keeping the sum of the losses constant. This is a shift in thinking you must make.

Thinking in this way sets you up nicely to think in terms of odds, because in chaotic systems all you can bank on are odds playing out in the long run. For example, if you flip a coin, do you know in advance whether it's going to be a heads or tails? Probably not. But if someone asked you to predict the distribution of heads versus tails over 10,000 flips, you could reasonably guess that it'll be 5000 heads and 5000 tails. You might be off by a few flips either way, but you'll be pretty close percentage-wise.

In fact, the greater the number of flips, the lesser your error percentage. This is because the odds inherent in a pattern that occurs in a chaotic system express themselves best over the long run. Your trading strategy is precisely such a pattern. The market is a chaotic system. Hence, you should focus on executing your strategy as it is meant to be executed over and over again and worry about profitability only in the long run.

Contrast this with the usual attitude of traders who seek to win every single trade. This is impossible to accomplish since no trading strategy or pattern is correct 100% of the time. If we were discussing directional strategies, I'd spend a lot more time on this, but the fact is that options take care of a lot of this ambiguity themselves.

This is because you don't have to do much when trading options. You enter and then monitor the trade. Sure, it helps to have some directional bias, but even if you get it wrong, your losses will be extremely limited, and you're more likely to hit winners than losers.

Despite this, always think of your strategy in terms of its odds. There are two basic metrics to measure this. The first is the win rate of your system. This is simply the percentage of winners you have. The second is your payout ratio which is the average win size divided by the average loss size.

Together these two metrics will determine how profitable your system is. Both of them play off one another, and an increase in one is usually met by a decrease in another. It takes an extremely skillful trader to increase both simultaneously.

Risk Per Trade

The quantitative side of risk management when it comes to options trading is lesser than what you need to take care of when trading directionally. However, this doesn't mean there's nothing to worry about. Perhaps the most important metric of them all is your risk per trade. The risk per trade is what ultimately governs your profitability.

How much should you risk per trade? Common wisdom says that you should restrict this to 2% of your capital. For options trading purposes, this is perfectly fine. In fact, once you build your skill and can see opportunities better, I'd suggest increasing it to a higher level.

A point that you must understand here is that you must keep your risk per trade consistent for it to have any effect. You might see a wonderful setup and think that it has no chance of failure, but the truth is that you don't know how things will turn out. Even the prettiest setup has every chance of failing, and the ugliest setup you can think of may result in a profit. So never adjust your position size based on how something looks.

Calculating your position size for a trade is a pretty straightforward task. Every option's strategy will have a fixed maximum risk amount. Divide the capital risk by this amount, and that gives you your position size. Round that down to the nearest whole number since you can only buy whole number lots when it comes to contract sizes.

For example, let's say your maximum risk is $50 per lot on the trade. Your capital is $10,000. Your risk per trade is 2%. So the amount you're risking on that trade is 2% of 10,000 which is $200. Divide this by 50, and you get 4. Hence, your position size is four contracts or 400 shares. (You'll buy the contracts, not the shares.)

Why is it important to keep your risk per trade consistent? Well, recall that your average win and loss size is important when it comes to determining your profitability. These, in conjunction with your strategy's success rate, determine how much money you'll make. If you keep shifting your risk amount per trade, you'll shift your win and loss sizes. You might argue that since it's an average, you can always adjust amounts to reflect an average.

My counter to that is how would you know which trades to adjust in advance? You won't know which ones are going to be a win or a loss, so you won't know which trade sizes to adjust to meet the average. Hence, keep it consistent across all trades and let the math work for you.

Aside from risk per trade, there are some simple metrics you should keep track of as part of your quantitative risk management plan.

Drawdown

A drawdown refers to the reduction in capital your account experiences. Drawdowns by themselves always occur. The metrics you should be measuring are the maximum drawdown and recovery period. If you think of your account's balance as a curve, the maximum drawdown is the biggest peak to trough distance in dollars. The recovery period is the subsequent time it took for your account to make new equity high.

If your risk per trade is far too high, your max drawdown will be unacceptably high. For example, if you risk 10% per trade and lose two in a row, which is very likely, your drawdown is going to be 20%. This is an absurdly large hole to dig your way out.

Consider that your capital has decreased by 20% and the subsequent climb back up needs to be done on lesser capital than previously.

This is why you need to keep your risk per trade low and in line with your strategy's success rate. The best way to manage drawdowns and limit the damage they cause is to put in place risk limits per day, week, and month. Even professional athletes who train to do one thing all the time have bad days, so it's unfair to expect yourself to be at 100% all the time.

These risk limits will take you out of the game when you're playing poorly. A daily risk limit is to prevent you from getting into a spiral of revenge trading. A good limit to stick to when starting off is to stop trading if you experience three losses in a row. This is pretty unlikely with options trades to be honest unless you screw up badly, but it's good to have a limit in place from a perspective of discipline.

Aim for a maximum weekly drawdown limit of 5% and a monthly drawdown limit of 6-8%. These are pretty high limits, to be honest, and if you are a directional trader, these limits do not apply to you. Directional traders need to be a lot more conservative than options trader when it comes to risk.

Understand that these are hard stop limits. So if your account has hit its monthly drawdown level within the first week, you need to take the rest of the month off. Overtrading and a lack of reflection on progress can cause a lot of damage, and a drawdown is simply a reflection of that.

Qualitative Risk

Quantitative metrics aside, your ability to properly manage qualitative things in your life and trading will dictate a lot of your success. Prepare well, and you're likely to see progress. You need to see preparation as your responsibility. I mean, no one else can prepare for you can they?

There are different elements to tracking your level of preparation so let's look at them one by one.

Health

You can't trade if you're physically unfit. If you have a fever or if you're suffering from some condition that makes it impossible for you to concentrate, forget about trading. You can rest assured that the other traders in the market will be more than happy to take your money.

When viewed from an options trading perspective, the risk is even more acute. All options strategies will require you to write options at some point, even the most basic ones like in this book. Even if your position is covered, making a mistake, and having an option you wrote be exercised by the buyer is an unpleasant thing that happens. Maintain a regimen of exercise and eat healthy food.

Depending on how long you sit in front of your screen, you might even want to consider avoiding certain foods when in session.

Heavy meals and food that makes you drowsy will cause your performance to dip, so avoid eating them when you're in the market. Also, don't exercise to such an extent that you're completely exhausted. The idea is to be fresh and alert, not fatigued and aching for a good sleep.

You might have an image of traders as being highly wired and as people who spend their entire lives in front of a screen. Well, most traders do sit in front of a screen most of the time, but the successful ones make time for other stuff in their lives as well. So don't try to copy some false vision here. Instead, do what feels comfortable to you while taking care to not slip into habits that are detrimental to your success.

Lifestyle

Your fitness is just one part of your lifestyle, of course. Is your lifestyle conducive to profitable trading? Are you someone who loves staying up at all sorts of odd hours and considers it perfectly normal to stumble onto a work task while hungover or worse? Make no mistake, the market will make you donate all of your capital to it.

Many beginners underestimate how difficult trading is. This should come as no surprise since beginners by definition underestimate anything. What shocks most of them is the degree to which they underestimate the difficulty of trading successfully. Let me put it in writing for you: Trading is one of the most challenging things you will ever do in your life.

The reason it is so difficult is due to the ever-changing nature of the market and the mental demands it places upon you. Another key lifestyle question to consider is the hours when you'll trade. Most of you reading this probably have full-time jobs and cannot spend your whole day in front of the market.

So plan out when you'll trade and how you'll prepare yourself for the session. What routines will you carry out? If you're going to trade in the morning before work begins, how will you manage to do this? Will you work in a quiet place or in some noisy truck stop on the way to work? Options positions don't need a lot of maintenance, so there's not much need for this, but when will you check in on the market throughout the day? Will you check in a few times? Five times? Define everything to do with your routine.

Think of yourself as a professional athlete who has to show up for a game everyday. An athlete has a precise method of preparation before showing up for a game. They don't deviate from their preparatory routine and certainly don't experiment with new things during game time. Practice is when they try out new stuff.

How will you practice your skills and improve your ability to execute your strategy? When will you do this? Plan it all out and develop your success routine.

Mental States

Trading is a mental activity. You don't need to lift or push anything physically. Therefore it is crucial to ensure that your mental state is as optimal as it needs to be for you to execute properly. Having a checklist or a mental check-in list works wonders for the trading process.

Before any trading, write down what's going through your mind and ask yourself how you feel. If you find that you're tired or frustrated and unable to focus properly, step away, and do not trade. If you're planning on sitting in front of your terminal for more than an hour, make it a habit to check in with yourself every half hour or hourly. This need not be a detailed examination, just a simple check-in with yourself to see how things are going.

Take your risk management tasks seriously, and the market will reward you with profits. Do not be the trader who stumbles into the market completely unprepared and then wonders why trading is so unforgiving. Above all else, seek to eliminate all sources of stress when it comes to trading. Take regular breaks and schedule months off from the market to recap and assimilate the things you've learned and need to improve.

Trading every single day of the year does not make sense. This isn't a job where you'll be rewarded with a certain salary for just showing up. You need to produce results, and in order to do so, you need to manage your downside carefully.

An excellent practice is to review how you work and set aside months exclusively for trading and months exclusively for practice purposes. By practice, I mean reviewing your prior results, working on your mindset and improving your risk management abilities. This is an unconventional method of working but it will pay massive dividends down the line.

Now that you have a better understanding of the basics, it's finally time to jump in and take a look at various trading strategies you can deploy with options.

BUILDING A PORTFOLIO

The ideal portfolio should contain between 25 and 30 different securities. This is the perfect way of ensuring that the risk levels are drastically reduced and the only expected outcomes are profitability.

Diversification is a popular strategy that is used by both traders and investors. It makes use of a wide variety of securities in order to improve yield and mitigate against inherent and potential risks.

It is advisable to invest or trade in a variety of assets and not all from one class. For instance, a properly diversified portfolio should include assets such as currencies, options, stocks, bonds, and so on. This approach will increase the chances of profitability and minimize risks and exposure. Diversification is even better if assets are acquired across geographical regions as well.

Best Diversification Approach

Diversification focuses on asset allocation. It consists of a plan that endeavors to allocate funds or assets appropriately across a variety of investments. When an investor diversifies his or her portfolio, then there is some level of risk that has to be accepted. However, it is also advisable to devise an exit strategy so that the investor is able to let go of the asset and recoup their funds. This becomes necessary when a specific asset class is not yielding any worthwhile returns compared to others.

If an investor is able to create an aptly diversified portfolio, their investment will be adequately covered. An adequately diversified portfolio also allows room for growth. Appropriate asset allocation is highly recommended as it allows investors a chance to leverage risk and manage any possible portfolio volatility because different assets have varying reactions to adverse market conditions.

Investor opinions on diversifications

Different investors have varying opinions regarding the type of investment scenarios they consider being ideal. Numerous investors believe that a properly diversified portfolio will likely bring in a double-digit return despite prevailing market conditions. They also agree that in the worst-case situation will be simply a general decrease in the value of the different assets. Yet with all this information out there, very few investors are actually able to achieve portfolio diversification.

So why are investors unable to simply diversify their portfolios appropriately? The answers are varied and diverse. The challenges encountered by investors in diversification include weighting imbalance, hidden correlation, underlying devaluation, and false returns, among others. While these challenges sound rather technical, they can easily be solved. The solution is also rather simple. By hacking these challenges, an investor will then be able to benefit from an aptly diversified platform.

The Process of Asset Class Allocation

There are different ways of allocating investments to assets. According to studies, most investors, including professional investors, portfolio managers, and seasoned traders actually rarely beat the indexes within their preferred asset class. It is also important to note that there is a visible correlation between the performance of an underlying asset class and the returns that an investor receives. In general, professional investors tend to perform more or less the same as an index within the same class asset.

Investment returns from a diversified portfolio can generally be expected to closely imitate the related asset class. Therefore, asset class choice is considered an extremely crucial aspect of an investment. In fact, it is the single more crucial aspect for the success of a particular asset class. Other factors, such as individual asset selection and market timing, only contribute about 6% of the variance in investment outcomes.

Wide Diversifications between Various Asset Classes

Diversification to numerous investors simply implies spreading their funds through a wide variety of stocks in different sectors such as health care, financial, energy, as well as medium caps, small, and large-cap companies. This is the opinion of your average investor. However, a closer look at this approach reveals that investors are simply putting their money in different sectors of stocks class. These asset classes can very easily fall and rise when the markets do.

A reliably diversified portfolio is one where the investor or even the manager is watchful and alert because of the hidden correlation that exists between different asset classes. This correlation can easily change with time, and there are several reasons for this. One reason is international markets. Many investors often choose to diversify their portfolios with international stocks.

However, there is also a noticeable correlation across the different global financial markets. This correlation is clearly visible not just across European markets but also in emerging markets from around the world. There is also a clear correlation between equities and fixed income markets, which are generally the hallmarks of diversification.

This correlation is actually a challenge and is probably a result of the relationship between structured financing and investment banking. Another factor that contributes to this correlation is the rapid growth and popularity of hedge funds. Take the case where a large international organization such as a hedge fund suffers losses in a particular asset class.

Should this happen, then the firm may have to dispose of some assets across the different asset classes. This will have a multiplier effect as numerous other investments, and other investors will, therefore, be affected even though they had diversified their portfolios appropriately. This is a challenge that affects numerous investors who are probably unaware of its existence. They are also probably unaware of how it should be rectified or avoided.

Realignment of Asset Classes

One of the best approaches to solving the correlation challenge is to focus on class realignment. Basically, asset allocation should not be considered as a static process. Asset class imbalance is a phenomenon that occurs when the securities markets develop, and different asset classes exhibit varied performance.

After a while, investors should assess their investments then diversify out of underperforming assets and instead shift this investment to other asset classes that are performing well and are profitable in the long term. Even then, it is advisable to be vigilant so that no one single asset class is over-weighted as other standard risks are still inherent. Also, a prolonged bullish market can result in overweighting one of the different asset classes which could be ready for a correction.

Diversification and the Relative Value

Investors sometimes find asset returns to be misleading, including veteran investors. As such, it is advisable to interpret asset returns in relation to the specific asset class performance. The interpretation should also take into consideration the risks that this asset class is exposed to and even the underlying currency.

When diversifying investments, it is important to think about diversifying into asset classes that come with different risk profiles. These should also be held in a variety of currencies. You should not expect to enjoy the same outcomes when investing in government bonds and technology stocks. However, it is recommended to endeavor to understand how each suits the larger investment objective.

Using such an approach, it will be possible to benefit more from a small gain from an asset within a market where the currency is increasing in value. This is as compared to a large gain from an asset within a market where the currency is in decline. As such, huge gains can translate into losses when the gains are reverted back to the stronger currency. This is the reason why it is advisable to ensure that proper research and evaluation of different asset classes are conducted.

Currencies should be considered

Currency considerations are crucial when selecting asset classes to diversify in. take the Swiss franc for instance. It is one of the world's most stable currencies and has been that way since the 1940s. Because of this reason, this particular currency can be safely and reliably used to measure the performance of other currencies.

However, private investors sometimes take too long to choose and trading stocks. Such activities are both overwhelming and time-consuming. This is why, in such instances, it is advisable to approach this differently and focus more on the asset class. With this kind of approach, it is possible to be even more profitable. Proper asset allocation is crucial to successful investing. It enables investors to mitigate any investment risks as well as portfolio volatility. The reason is that different asset classes have different reactions to all the different market conditions.

Constructing a well-thought-out and aptly diversified portfolio, it is possible to have a stable and profitable portfolio that even outperforms the index of assets. Investors also have the opportunity to leverage against any potential risks because of different reactions by the different market conditions.

An Example

An investor has a total of $100,000 to invest. The best approach is to put the funds in a diversified portfolio, but the challenge is properly or adequately balancing the portfolio. The first step is to check out market conditions and then conduct an assessment of possible returns versus any likely risks. As such, the investor can choose to invest in very secure investments that are likely to produce long-term income.

Such an investment can include between 10 and 12 stocks that are highly diversified. These are generally stocks from different sectors, industries, and countries. This kind of diversification helps to leverage against any possible risks and also ensures the portfolio is thoroughly mixed.

Portfolio Diversification Approach

Disciplined Investing is a Must

Everyone is in agreement that diversification is basically the right approach. However, as an investor, there is a need to be disciplined even as you invest and diversify your investments. Investing is an art form. Put your money in equities but not all your money. Instead, think of yourself as a mutual fund manager then come up with a list of companies to invest in. You can also invest in funds and trusts like REITs or real estate investment trusts and exchange-traded funds. It is also advisable to go beyond local borders and invest globally. This way, you spread your risk around and stand chances of enjoying much better returns.

Consider Investing in Bonds and Index Funds

Apart from investing in stocks across numerous sectors, a trader may also want to invest your funds in certain fixed-income or index funds. When you invest in securities that closely keep an eye on a major index is highly recommended as you will be able to monitor progress and known when to make adjustments and so on. Such funds charge very low fees, and you will be able to easily track your investments.

Portfolio Building is a Continuous Process

Try to always grow your investments. If you receive some cash from somewhere, you can consider investing part or the entire amount into your investment portfolio. Also, keep adding regular amounts to your portfolio. You can, for instance, add about $500 each month to this portfolio to grow it at a much faster pace.

Learn the Best Exit Times

Sometimes we tend to get comfortable with the purchase-and-hold approach. This is true, especially when our investments are on autopilot. Yet a smart investor you need to keep looking out for events and special moments. Always remain abreast of events and be ready to act depending on the nature of the event. This way, you will be prepared for the moment when you have to cut your losses and exit your trades.

Watch Out for Commissions

As a trader, you need to remember that there are commissions to be paid as well as fees and charges. These charges can add up over time and become a significant amount. Therefore, keep a lookout for the charges and ensure that they are always maintained at manageable levels. In general, investing should be informative, fun, rewarding, and educational.

However, you need to be disciplined as a trader in order to be profitable in the long term and possibly outperform some of the major indices. Apart from the buy-and-hold strategy, you should diversify your portfolio, keep growing your portfolio, and learn to read the signs and know when the time is right to exit a trade. This way, your trading ventures will become extremely fruitful in the long run.

Diversification Summary

Diversification can easily be summed up using a single phrase. Never put all your eggs in one basket. This is as simple as it gets. However, the statement does not explain exactly how to go about diversification.

The idea behind portfolio diversification is simple. A trader needs to diversify into a whole group of securities, and these should be from different asset classes. It would be wrong for a portfolio to contain only stocks from one company only. Should anything happen to that company, then the investor or even trader stands to suffer huge losses, and such losses can end the investment or trade dreams of a trader.

When an investment is split into two or more different companies and asset classes, then the potential risk facing a certain product is drastically reduced. Apart from investing in more than one company, it is also a great idea to put funds in other securities such as bonds, futures, and currencies.

Traders need to develop an asset allocation strategy. Such a strategy should mostly focus on investment in stocks and bonds. Asset allocation is closely related to diversification because when done properly, asset allocation leads to a sustainably diversified portfolio.

There are other additions that can secure a portfolio and improve its diversification. These include mutual funds that consist of varied securities. A mutual fund is generally a diversified investment so diversifying into a fund helps in further diversification of a portfolio.

It is advisable to learn how to arrive at a desirable risk to reward ratio. Such a ratio can help determine the best way to diversify funds. A risk-reward ratio provides the opportunity to enjoy a particular rate of return for those willing to assume a small level of risk. Therefore, those willing to take on higher risk levels are more likely to benefit more compared to those assuming lower levels of risk.

There are some who prefer lower risk levels because perhaps of their limited resources or perhaps they prefer minimal complications. Such investors simply mirror a single and balanced fund. Others choose to simply invest in the fund. However, this can be viewed as simplistic by others who may wish for a more diversified approach.

In conclusion, diversification is key for sustainable investment, especially in the long run. It is not just more profitable but provides a risk management element into the entire investment portfolio process. Finding a suitable balance in the choice of assets provides a great approach to apt diversification.

Day Trading

When you're day trading, you're going to buy and sell a stock within one day, and do so without waiting for close. A day trader is looking for stocks that have short term volatility. Of course, you're going to want to buy low and sell high. Although day traders are viewed by the general public as gamblers, this is far from reality. A day trader is using reasoned strategies to make profits. Of course, some day traders are better than others, they have more experience, they may study the markets better, and have a better sense of timing. However, things don't always go as planned, so day trading does carry a lot more risk than simply buying into stocks for the long term.

Smart Money vs. Dumb Money

There are two general types of investors. The first is institutional investors. These are large investors like pension funds and hedge funds. Institutional investors are colloquially known as "smart money". They are called smart money because they have more information available and have tools at their disposal like Bloomberg terminals which cost a lot of money while giving them rapid information. Also controlling huge amounts of capital, they can even move the markets.

Retail investors are individual and small traders. This is the "dumb money" – in other words, that is you. Don't take offense, the term doesn't really mean that you are dumb in the sense of being stupid! Dumb money just means that relatively speaking, compared to the large institutional investors you don't have access to the same information at the same speed, so you're not going to be making trades that are as well-informed.

Selling short

Let's begin by looking at a strategy known as selling short. This strategy relies on being able to borrow shares from a broker so that you can profit on the share price decline. The process involves the following steps. First, you'll borrow shares from the broker. Then you sell them on the market. When the share price drops, then you'll buy the shares again, and then you return the shares to the broker.

Of course, this depends on things going in your favor. If the share price doesn't drop, you risk losing money.

To see how you could profit from this, we'll use a simple example. Let's say that ABC is trading at $20 a share at market opening. They're going to release a quarterly report and you're expecting bad news that will make the share price drop, at least for a while. You borrow 100 shares from the broker, and then you immediately sell them. So, you make:

$20 x 100 = $2,000

At this point, it's borrowed money since you must return the shares to the broker. If you're wrong and the price goes up, then you're going to have a loss. But let's say the news comes out and as you expected its very bad news. Say the share price drops to $14. Now you can buy 100 shares at this lower price:

$14 x 100 = $1,400

Then you immediately return the shares to the broker. So, you've made a profit given by:

Price you sold the borrowed shares – Price you paid to get them back = $2,000 - $1,400 = $600 profit.

Scalping

Chances are you're familiar with the concept of scalping tickets to an upcoming event, maybe a music concert or high demand sporting event. The idea is you buy the tickets at face value, then when it's sold out you show up at the venue and offer your tickets for sale at a premium price to make a profit.

Scaling isn't the same on the stock market, but scalping is the most basic strategy used by day traders. At its core is the notion of "buy low, sell high". When a day trader uses scalping, they buy the shares at a given price, and then sell immediately when they stand to make a profit. So, if you buy 100 shares of ABC company for $10 a share, a total investment of $10 x 100 = $1,000, you then closely monitor the share price to sell when it becomes profitable. Suppose that at first, it drops to $9.50 a share, and bounces around a bit. Then it jumps up to $11.75 a share. At this point you'll sell right away, earning:

100 shares x $11.75/share = $1,175

Stop loss points

A stop loss is a point that is chosen as a kind of insurance to limit losses incurred on security. This is done with a stop-loss order. What you do is you place an order with the broker to buy or sell the stock when it reaches a certain price. As an example, suppose you buy XYZ stock at $100. After you purchase the shares, you can place a stop-loss order for $95. What this does is your shares will be sold if the price drops to $95. That protects you from incurring even more losses if the stock is tanking.

The buy signal

The point of doing these calculations is to determine when to buy, when to sell, and when to cut your losses. The buy signal occurs when the price of the stock goes above the pivot point with conviction. You are bullish on the stock, expecting the price to keep rising (it may not). Your first profit target is given by R1.

For our case, the pivot point was $99.67. If the price breaks strongly above this, we take that as a buy signal. The previous days close was $100 so we will say for this example that the share price jumped to $101. We could decide to buy the shares at this price.

The profit point is R1, which is $102.34 based on our calculations. You could choose to sell if the stock price hits R1. However, if the stock is rising rapidly, then you can choose R2 as your profit target. In that case, you would wait until the price hits $104.67 to sell.

If you are right, then you purchased shares of XYZ stock at $101 per share. If we buy 100 shares, then we are in for:

100 x $101 = $10,100

Now suppose that it does hit R2. We immediately sell, so our gross revenue is:

100 x $104.67 = $10,467

We've made a profit of $10,467 - $10,100 = $367. If that was the only trade, we made that day, then we've made a pretty nice daily income of $367.

Of course, things don't always go as planned, which is why you need a stop loss point. You do this so that you can minimize losses and avoid losing your shirt. Whether you stick to R1 or R2 as the point at which you'll sell for a profit or not will depend on how rapidly the stock is going up. So, you'll be looking at a measure of its momentum. The stop loss points S1 and S2 correspond to each case. For R1, which is $102.34, your stop loss point would be S1 = $97.33. If the stock is shooting up and immediately goes above R1, you can take P as your stop loss. If it has gone up to R1 but doesn't show more conviction (i.e. that it's going to go up to R2) then you sell at about R1 and take the smaller profits.

Morning or Opening Gaps

A morning gap is when a stock opens higher or lower than it closed the previous day. Suppose that XYZ stock closed at $50. If it opens the next morning it opens at $51, then this would be a $1 gap up. On the other hand, if the stock opened at $49.50, that would be a 50-cent gap down.

A strategy that day traders use is called fade the gap. There are two options:

- If the stock opens up, take a short position.
- If the stock opens down, take a long position.

The bet while using this strategy is that the stock is going to return to a value near the previous days close. This is called filling the gap. In other words, you're betting on the opposite trend the stock had at the opening of the markets.

With options trading:

- If the stock opens up, you'll buy puts on the stock.

- If the stock opens down, you'll buy calls on the stock.

Here is an example. On April 18, 2019, Apple closed at $203.86 a share. The markets were closed on Friday for Easter, on Monday, April 22, 2019, Apple opened at $202.65 a share.

Since the stock opened lower than the previous day's close, you'd take a long position on the stock, hoping that it would close the gap and rise back up to the closing price. You could buy stock and hold it until it (hopefully) rose to a profitable point, or you could buy call options on the stock. Looking at what the stock did, we see that had we bought call options on Apple at the beginning of the trading day, this would have been successful speculation. By 4 PM the stock had closed at $204.53 a share. But as a day trader, you would have closed your position using this technique when it had gotten back to the previous days close.

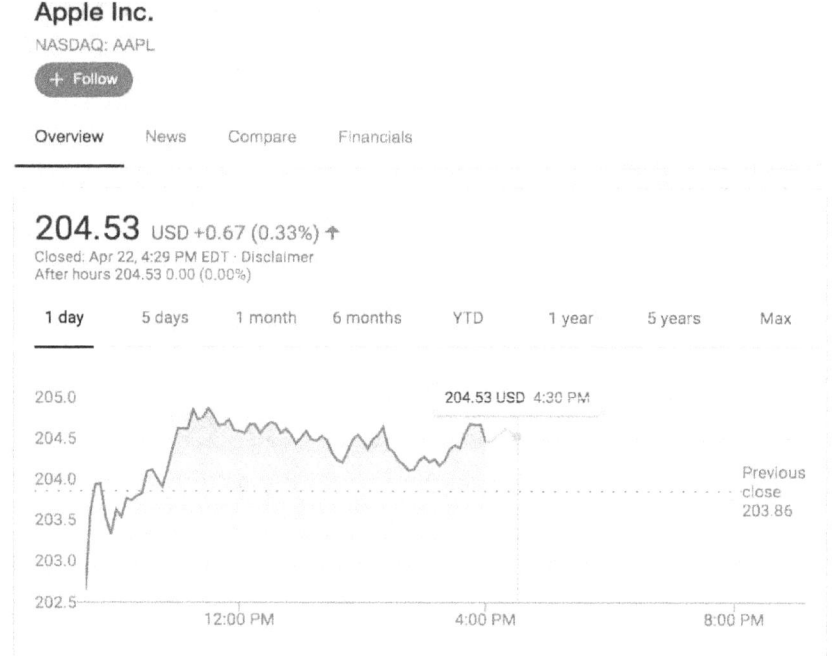

This was a fortuitous example since the stock happened to go significantly above the previous close and stayed up most of the day. Of course, this is a risky venture, since that is not always going to be something that works out.

However, the data indicate that it is actually a fairly reasonable approach. Most stocks to fill the gap at some point during the following trading day. It's estimated that 68% of stocks will completely fill the gap, and 78% will fill the gap at least half-way. You're making a decent bet that will be right most of the time. There is some risk in that if you're waiting for it to fill the gap completely and it's at the half-way point, that it doesn't get to where you're hoping it will go and end up trading without maximizing potential profits.

Fading

Fading is a bet against dumb money in the stock market. The technique is based on shorting stocks that have moved upward rapidly, typically in the first hour after market open. The idea is based on the belief that the stock is overbought, that is retail investors have jumped in on stock and bid up to the price based on some news about the stock. During the process, eager retail investors will bid the price up beyond its intrinsic value, so as the trading day goes on the price will begin dropping.

The point to get in and short the stock is to look for when the upswing begins slowing down or fading. Obviously, fading is a high-risk strategy, you don't have the same information available as the institutional investors so may be guessing wrong even when it appears that the rise of the stock is sputtering. You should always protect yourself with a stop-loss.

Candlesticks

A candlestick is a marking on a stock chart or graph that represents the following four data points:

- Open

- High

- Low

- Close

-

Candlesticks are colored red or green on a chart. Just for the sake of seeing a representation, here is a screenshot of a couple of candlesticks for a specific stock:

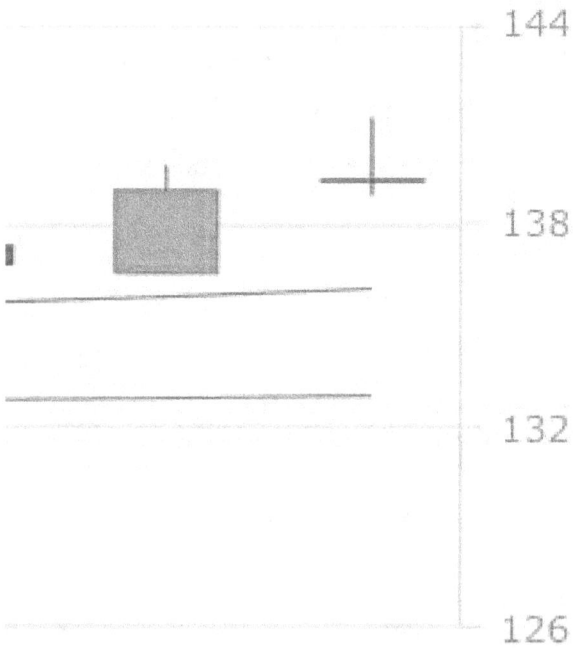

Candlesticks can be green or red in color. The rectangle shown on the chart is the body of the candlestick. If the candlestick is green, the bottom represents the opening price, and the top represents the closing price. The narrow lines emanating from the candlestick body are called the wicks. If the candlestick is green color, that means the price of the stock went up over the given time period. If you have a monthly chart, then the green color indicates that by the close of the day, for that day the stock went up in price.

A red candlestick indicates that the price of the stock went up for the period of measurement. If the time period is one month, then the top indicates the opening price, while the bottom of the body indicates the opening price.

Let's illustrate this with pictures. Here is the candlestick when it is red in color on the chart:

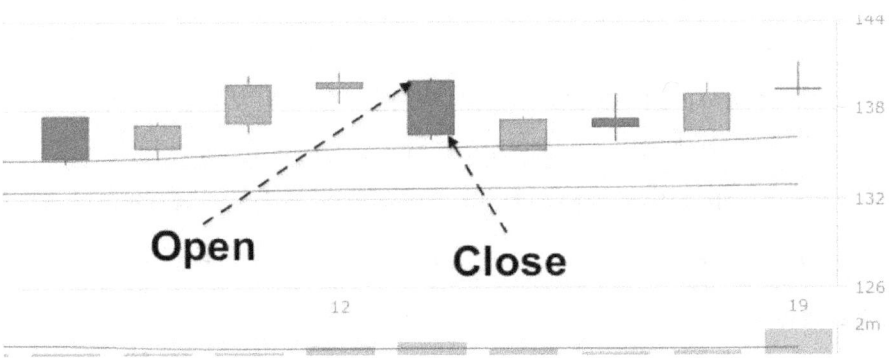

For a green candlestick, the chart representation is the opposite:

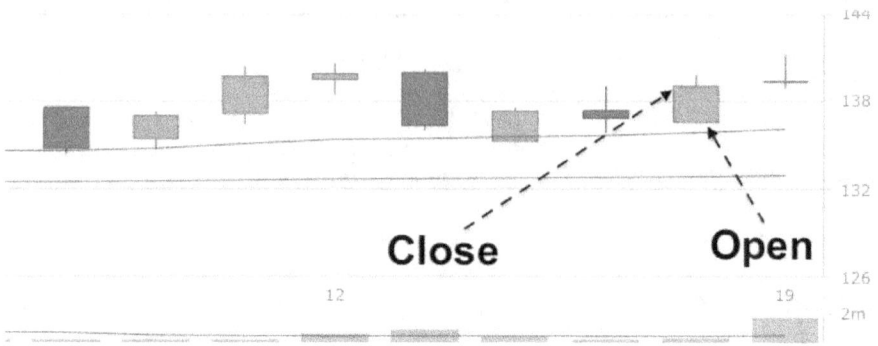

While the top and bottom of the body represent the open and close, the wicks are used to represent the high price, and the low price, respectively.

The top of the candlestick wick represents the high stock price for the day. The bottom of the wick represents the low price of the stock for the day. Or, if the time period is for one day, the ranges represent the change in price over five-minute intervals. So close is the price of the stock at the end of the five-minute period, while open is the price of the stock at the beginning of the five minute period.

Most often, when it comes to day trading, you're going to be looking at trading intervals for one single day so the prices represented will tell you how the stock moved over five-minute intervals:

- The high price of the stock over the five-minute interval.

- The low price of the stock over the five-minute interval.

- The closing or end price at the end of the five-minute interval.

- The opening or starting price of the stock over the five-minute interval.

When looking at candlestick charts, you're interested in knowing whether a bearish or bullish engulfing pattern presents itself. So, you pick a candlestick somewhere in the chart and compare that candlestick to the one to the left of the selected candlestick.

- If the candlestick on the right side is red and it engulfs or covers the entire range of the candlestick immediately to the left which is green (that is, the trading period five minutes prior), that is a bearish candlestick pattern. Remember that green means the price of the stock went up over the period. If the price goes down over the subsequent period (indicated by red color), then this is a bearish candlestick. If this occurs at the top of an uptrend, then this is considered a reversal candle.

Here, we have red followed by green at the bottom of a downturn. The green candlestick to the right, which completely covers the red candlestick to the left, is said to engulf the red candlestick. If you are long, this is a good sign. This indicates a reversal, so the stock price can be expected to increase.

On the other hand, suppose we have a red candle that engulfs a green candle. The red is to the right:

If you are shorting a stock, this is a good sign. Otherwise, it's a bad sign. This indicates a reversal if you are at the top of an upturn. That is, the larger red candle which engulfs the green candle to the left (i.e. earlier in time) indicates that the stock is in reversal, which means that the stock is heading to a downturn. If you are long on the stock, it's a bad sign. If you are shorting the stock, or invested in puts, that means that it's a good sign, i.e. that the stock can be expected to be heading into a downturn.

- If you see several red candles heading down in a downturn, and then you see a green candle that engulfs the previous red candle, this is bullish – so may indicate a coming upturn on the stock price. So if you are bullish on the stock, this indicates a buying opportunity if you are long, or if you want to buy calls.

- If you see several green candles going up, and then there is a red candle the engulfs the previous (to the left) green candle, then this is bearish, that is we expect a downturn in the stock price. If you are buying puts, this is the time to buy.

These are guidelines, but not rules. So, while it might be accurate, it's not going to be accurate all the time.

A shooting star or "inverted hammer" is a candlestick with the top wick much longer than the bottom wick.

These are reversal candles, so are important to recognize in charts. In the chart below, notice that the candle has little or no wick below it, and it has a small body with a long wick above.

The candle is red in color. This indicates that it is a bearish candle. This is a sell signal if you are long in the stock, or if you are looking to short, that is a buy signal.

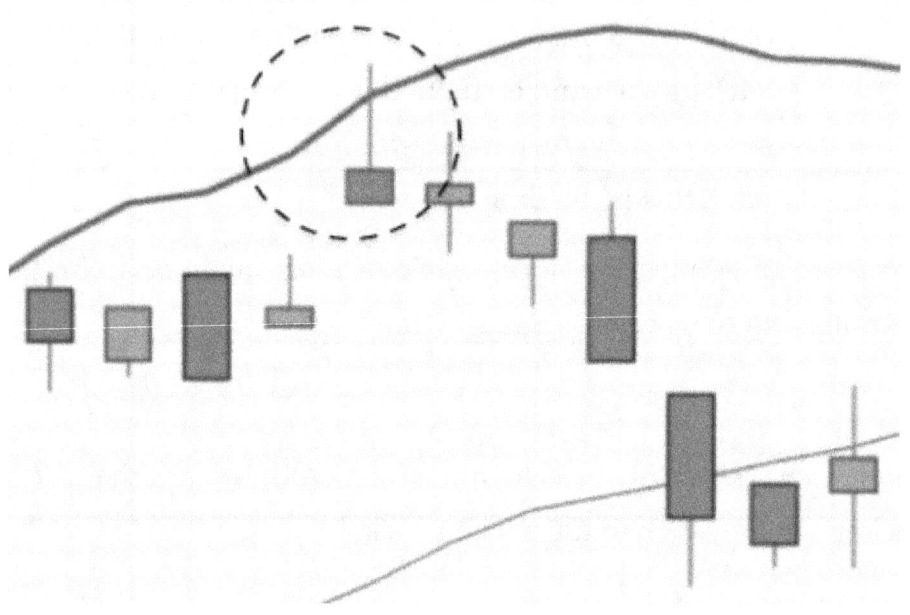

BEGINNERS COMMON MISTAKES

If you can avoid these mistakes when you are just getting started, you will be way ahead of the pack and will also save yourself a lot of losses and misery. Write down these "5 Commandments" on a sticky note and put it on your computer screen:

1. Don't buy stocks that are hitting 52-week lows.
2. Don't trade penny stocks.
3. Don't short stocks.
4. Don't trade on margin.
5. Don't trade other people's ideas.

1. Don't buy stocks that are hitting 52-week lows.

So many new traders lose a lot of money trying to catch the proverbial "falling knife." In spite of what everyone will tell you, you are almost always much better off buying a stock that is hitting 52-week highs than one hitting 52-week lows.

When a stock goes down a lot, it can affect the company's fundamentals as well. Employee and management morale will deteriorate, the best employees may leave the company, and it may become more difficult for the company to raise money by selling shares or issuing debt.

Conversely, when a stock goes up a lot, it can improve the company's fundamentals. Employee and management morale will be high, everyone at the company will want to work harder, it will be easier to recruit new talent, and it will become easier for the company to raise money by issuing stock or debt.

If you stick to stocks that are trading above their 200-day moving averages, or that are hitting 52-week highs, you will do much better than trying to catch falling knives.

2. Don't trade penny stocks.

A penny stock is any stock that trades under $5. Unless you are an advanced trader, you should avoid all penny stocks. I would extend this by encouraging you to also avoid all stocks priced under $10.

Even if you have a small trading account ($5,000) or less, you are better off buying fewer shares of a higher-priced stock than a lot of shares of a penny stock.

That is because low-priced stocks are most often associated with lower quality companies. As a result, they are not usually allowed to trade on the NYSE or the Nasdaq. Instead, they trade on the OTCBB ("over the counter bulletin board") or Pink Sheets, both of which have much less stringent financial reporting requirements than the major exchanges do.

Many of these companies have never made a profit. They may be frauds or shell companies that are designed solely to enrich management and other insiders. They may also include former "blue chips" that have fallen on hard times like Eastman Kodak or Lehman Brothers.

In addition, penny stocks are inherently more volatile than higher-priced stocks. Think of it this way: if a $100 stock moves $1, that is a 1% move. If a $5 stock moves $1, that is a 20% move. Many new traders underestimate the kind of emotional and financial damage that this kind of volatility can cause.

In my experience, penny stocks do not trend nearly as well as higher-priced stocks. They tend to be more mean-reverting (Mean reversion occurs when a stock moves up sharply from its average trading price, only to fall right back down again to its average trading price). Many of them are eventually headed to zero, but they are still not good short candidates. Most brokers will not let you short them. And even if you do find a broker who will let you short a penny stock, how would you like to wake up to see your penny stock trading at $10 when you just shorted it at $2 a few days before? I learned that lesson the hard way. It turned out that I was risking $8 to make $2, which is not a good way to make money over the long term.

To add injury to insult, a penny stock might appear to be liquid one day, and the next day, the liquidity dries up and you are confronted by a $2 bid/ask spread. Or the bid might completely disappear. Imagine owning a stock for which there are now no buyers.

Stay away from all stocks under $10. Also stay away from trading newsletters that hawk penny stocks. The owners of these newsletters are often paid by the companies themselves to hype their stocks. Or they may take a position in a penny stock, send out an email telling everyone to buy it, and then sell their stock at a much higher price to these amateur buyers.

Watch the movie "The Wolf of Wall Street" if you'd like to see a famous example of the decadent lifestyle and fraud that often surround penny stocks. Viewer discretion is advised.

3. Don't short stocks.

If you are an advanced trader, feel free to ignore this rule. If you are not, I would seriously encourage you not to ignore this rule.

In order to short a stock, you must first borrow shares of the stock from your broker. You then sell those shares on the open market. If the stock falls in price, you will be able to buy back those shares at a lower price for a profit. If, however, the stock goes up a lot, you may be forced to buy back the shares at a much higher price, and end up losing more money than you ever had in your trading account to begin with.

In November 2015, Joe Campbell broke 2 of the 5 commandments. He first decided to trade a penny stock called KaloBios Pharmaceuticals. To make things worse, he decided to short it.

When he went to bed that evening, his trading account was worth roughly $37,000. When he woke up the next morning, the stock had skyrocketed. As a result, not only had he lost all of the $37,000, but he now owed his broker an additional $106,000.

And there was no way out. If you owe your broker money, they can haul you into court and go after your house and savings.

Sometimes even the wealthiest investors can be wiped out by shorting a stock. During the great Northern Pacific Corner of 1901, shares of that railroad stock went from $170 to $1,000 in a single day. That move bankrupted some of the wealthiest Americans of the day, who had shorted the stock and were then forced to cover at higher prices.

If you do end up shorting a stock, remember that your broker will charge you a fee (usually expressed as an annual interest rate) to borrow the stock. In addition, if you are short a stock, you are responsible for paying any dividends on that stock (your broker will automatically take the money out of your account quarterly).

For all of these reasons, shorting stocks is clearly an advanced and risky trading strategy. Don't try it until you've been trading for at least 5 years, and you have the financial stability to withstand a freakish upwards move in a stock.

And never short a penny stock. It's just not worth it.

4. Don't trade on margin.

In order to short a stock, you will need to open up a margin account with your broker, as Joe Campbell did. You'll also need a margin account in order to trade stocks using margin.

When you buy a stock on margin, it means that you are borrowing money from your broker, in order to purchase more shares of stock than you would normally be able to buy with just the cash sitting in your brokerage account.

Let's say that I have $10,000 in my margin account. Most brokers in the U.S. will allow me to go on margin to purchase $20,000 worth of stock in that account. What this means is that they are lending me an additional $10,000 (usually at some outrageous annual interest rate like 11%, which is what E*Trade currently charges) to buy more shares of stock.

If I buy $10,000 worth of stock and the stock goes up 10%, I've just made $1,000. But if I can increase the amount of stock that I'm buying to $20,000 using a margin loan, I will have made $2,000 on the same 10% move. That will mean that my trading account has just gone up by 20% ($2,000/$10,000).

Of course, if the stock goes down 10% and I'm on full margin, I will have lost 20% of my account value. Trading on margin is thus a form of leverage: it amplifies the performance of your portfolio both on the upside and the downside.

When you buy a stock using margin, the stock and cash in your trading account is held as collateral for the margin loan. If the stock falls enough, you may be required to add more cash to your account immediately (this is called "getting a margin call"), or risk having the broker force you to immediately sell your stock to raise cash. Often this will lead to your selling the stock at the worst possible time.

When you open up a new brokerage account and you are given the choice of a "cash account" or a "margin account," it's OK to pick "margin account." A margin account has certain advantages, such as being able to use the proceeds from selling a stock to immediately buy another stock without having to wait a few days for the trade to settle. If you never exceed your cash buying power in a margin account, you will never be charged fees or interest. In that way, it's quite possible to have a margin account, but never to go on margin.

If, however, you don't trust yourself, open up a "cash account." That way, you will never be allowed to trade on margin.

5. Don't trade other people's ideas.

There are two main reasons for this.

The first reason never to trade someone else's ideas is that they probably don't know what they are doing. If you get a hot stock tip from your neighbor or at the gym, it's best to ignore it. They probably have no idea what they are talking about.

Second, even if you get a really good and legitimate trading or investing idea from someone else, you will probably not have the conviction to hold on to it when the going gets tough. That conviction can only come from developing a trade idea yourself. When you have designed a trade, or researched an investment for yourself, you will have the conviction to hold on. You will also know where your stop loss is, in case the stock goes south. Have you noticed how hot stock tips never come with a recommended stop loss level?

Also, never place a trade based on something that you have just read in Barron's, Forbes, The Wall Street Journal, or have just seen on CNBC. Never buy a stock based on an analyst upgrade, or sell a stock based on an analyst downgrade.

I've seen analysts finally downgrade a stock only once it has fallen 50%. Analysts are lagging indicators. They tend to upgrade stocks that have already moved up, and downgrade stocks that have already moved down. There is also a strong selection bias among analysts. The best analysts get hired by hedge funds, and you never hear from them again. The worst analysts stay at the banks or brokerage houses, and continue to dispense their mediocre advice. Huge amounts of money have been lost by following their advice.

Should you even follow Warren Buffett's advice? Yes, and no. His advice is definitely much better than a hot stock tip from your neighbor. On the other hand, if you listened to him religiously, you missed out on all of the great tech stocks of the last 20 years. He waited until Apple and Amazon were up many thousands of percentage points before finally purchasing them.

Anyone can learn to think for themselves in the stock market, and come up with their own trading and investing ideas.

Rather than giving you a fish, I would much rather teach you how to fish for yourself. That is the path to true financial freedom.

HOW TO START OPTIONS TRADING

How Much Capital Is Needed?

After knowing how options trading works, do not rush to waste on your cash. There are too many risks in this type of trading. Capital is a basic requirement to start any business. Does options trading require too much capital? No. When starting on options trading, it is better to start with small capital to avoid massive trading risks.

Many are the individuals who utilize much of their cash for trading during their first days, which is so dangerous. Such individuals end up having too many risks to handle, and finally, they make up their minds to close their businesses. I do not want you to fall into such a mess. Do your thing with the right speed.

Start options trading with a reasonable small amount. Do not brag off that you got everything under control. You will lose even the only cash you had. Starting with less money has a high likelihood of fewer risks in trading. I bet you can now handle a few risks and be able to continue with your trading.

Strategies Used by Beginners for Options Trading

Options trading has a wide variety of strategies. There are simple to complex strategies that you can implement in options trading. Beginners find it tough to know the best simple strategies to utilize in their trading. You do not need to worry anymore. I have provided a detailed list below of the different simple options trading strategies you can use:

Buying calls. Buying calls is the simplest options trading strategy for beginners, investors, and even professionals. Investors prefer calls so much because this strategy provides them with the honor to purchase stock at a certain agreed price with a minimum amount of capital within an agreed time before its expiry.

Most of the bullish traders use this options strategy. When there is a rise in the price of the stock, you earn good profits. This strategy is right for any beginner who wants to generate better income, earn huge profits, and even save on the trading capital.

Its great potential to massive profits, however, makes it have a bigger exposure to the trading risks. You, as a buyer, can know the risks involved in your trading. Also, buying a call strategy has a better and secure feature, which can handle many risks.

The major drawback of purchasing calls is associated with the time of expiry and the loss of value. They always have a time of expiry, so you need to check on the timing. Call options lose their value when their time of expiry reaches. You do not earn any dividends when your options are past the date of expiry.

Buying put. Buying put is another simple strategy, which is just the vice versa of buying calls. Most investors use this expecting the stock's price will fall within that time before expiry. Investors always gain good enough profits when their prediction becomes right.

The things to put into consideration when buying put options include the time you are planning to be on trade and the amount of money you can afford to buy options. Purchase put options with at least one month remaining for them to expire. Do not purchase an option with a long duration before it expires. It will lose its time premium. You do not need to buy options with a duration like one year remaining for them to expire, because you will not wait to trade an option for a whole year. So, be wise when buying options.

The other consideration is all about buying options that you can afford. Do not torture yourself by buying expensive put options.

You will get hurt at the end. Weigh the different prices of the put options available and select the one you can afford according to the risks involved and the size of your account.

In case their prediction fails, the loss associated with this strategy is so limited. Unfortunately, you become exposed to so many risks.

Short put. Short put options strategy is all about buying a stock at a lower price than its current cost in the market. You gain profits in situations where the stock's price remains above an agreed price within that time of expiry. Otherwise, you incur many losses.

Conversely, in situations where the stock's price falls below the price agreed before the time of expiration, another party on trade sells you the stock at the agreed price, and you have to buy it no matter the cost.

Selling a short put option is quite simple, look for a margin account and a stock that will not drop its value any time soon. Select a date of expiration that is not that far and agree on the right price to generate more income when selling. By the time of expiry comes, you will earn good profits as long as the price does not fall.

You should be extra cautious when implementing this strategy, or else, you may lose value in your trading when things turn out unexpectedly.

Covered call. A covered call is one of the preferred options strategies for beginners. It is mostly suitable for traders who have expectations of small changes in the price of the stock or no changes at all within the expected time of expiry. A trader using this strategy normally purchases around 100 shares (unit of capital) of the stock and sells a call option against the unit of capital.

After selling the option, you acquire option premiums and decrease the cost of the share. If the price of the asset behaves unexpectedly in the market, meaning that it becomes greater than an agreed price, there should be the sale of the asset by the owner using the agreed price.

Married put. A married put is an options trading strategy quite similar to the insurance policies we normally have at our homes.

The strategy enables an investor who owns a stock, to purchase a put option on the stock to protect it against loss in value in the price of the stock.

You should buy the stock and put options on the same day. Also, you need to inform the options broker that the delivery of the stock you purchased will happen after the exercise of the put option. Marriage put strategy is normally used by bullish traders when buying their market trades who want to shield themselves from unlimited losses.

The drawback of this strategy is that it is costly to implement it on your trading portfolio.

Cash-secured put. On this strategy, traders write put options, and at the same time, put aside a sufficient amount of cash for buying stock. The benefits of this strategy are that you can decide on the price you want when you implement this strategy. Also, you receive payment of the options premiums when you sell cash-secured put options. In situations where the stock's price falls below an agreed price, the trader incurs too many losses.

Protective put. A protective put is an options trading strategy that many bullish traders implement to shield against loss of an asset, which is mostly caused by the drop in the price of an asset. A trader holds on to the long position of a stock and then buys a put option at an agreed price closer or equal to the price of the stock.

If it declines, the put options normally protect the agreed price (strike price) within that duration until the time of expiry. Remember, options have a date of expiration.

In scenarios where the price of the stock rises, the trader involved gains good enough profits. However, the profits reduce in cases of the options cost and also commissions. Another drawback of buying puts is that the total cost of the put normally surges due to the cost of the options.

You are supposed to offer the put options for sale in scenarios where the agreed price becomes greater than the stock's price after the time of expiry. However, this leaves the asset unprotected. Alternatively, a trader can also offer the put options for sale and purchase other options.

Collar strategy. Moderate bullish traders who formulate this strategy hold shares of an asset while at the same time, purchase put options and offer call options for sale. Both the put options and call options in collar strategy have a similar time of expiry.

It is also applicable to traders who are just writing covered calls to earn premiums and also want to protect themselves from the unexpected decline in the price of a stock.

A collar strategy normally limits losses in trading but also, unfortunately, limits the gaining of huge profits. You can make more profits without this strategy in cases where the price of the stock rises.

Now, with the idea of the simple options trading strategies that exist, you should sit down, think, and select the best strategy to use as a beginner. Weigh the risks and rewards of the strategy you will choose for excellent performance in options trading.

How to Start Options Trading

Now with the basic knowledge on options trading, I will provide you with a few details on how to start options trading journey.

1. You should look for an options trading broker. The key to successful options trading is your broker. There exist legit and non-legit brokers in options trading. Some of the tips for selecting a good broker include the following:

- Do some research on the broker first. You need to be keen and alert before opening a brokerage options trading platform. Different brokers will approach you with different platforms. Do not rush or assume everything is good; do some research on the best brokers. Make sure you spend your cash well by paying for a good options trading platform. It will help you a lot because your trading performance depends on your platform. Choose a broker with good ratings.

- Charges lower commissions. Some brokers tend to exploit traders by charging high commissions to beginners. You should weigh different commission offers of different brokers before settling on one. Some even charge no commission to traders. You should prefer brokers with fewer commissions. Payment of high commissions periodically can mess you up with losses, and you may find it even hard to secure your trading capital. Do not accept to pay high commissions. You also need to do some savings other than wasting money while paying commissions.

- A simple user interface platform. There is a wide variety of software with different functionalities and features. Some software has a simple user interface, while others are too complex for you to use. You should choose a platform with a simple and clear user interface that enables you to do your trades with less struggle. Some platforms can waste your precious time when you struggle too much searching on the Internet on how you operate them. Make your work easier by handling software that is according to your level.

- Trading tools for research. You should also consider factors like tools that are present on the platform. Do not purchase a platform with no tools. It will be hard for you. Platform tools ease your trading and make your performance excellent. The tools here may include charting tools, research tools, and even tools that alert you on any market changes that may arise.

- Do some testing on the brokerage platform. Do not be that kind of a careless trader who does things for the sake of doing with no precautions. You need to be cautious enough since this is an income-generating activity. You should test on a brokerage software before making up your mind of purchasing it. Check on the reliability and stability of the software and be 100% sure that this is the platform you will use for your trading. Ensure the software is not that type of platform that crashes down unexpectedly. You might miss crucial trade while fixing your software.

2. Be approved to trade options. You need to be approved by the broker in charge before purchasing and offering options for sale. They normally have their ways of approving you, like checking your experience and the money that you have. It aids in avoiding risks for the customers. You cannot escape this step.

3. Get a clear understanding of the technical analysis. Options trading is a technical field. You need to have the technical analysis techniques of trading options. The technical aspects include reading charts, know about the volume of stock, and also moving averages. Trading charts mostly analyze price behavior in the market. You will handle the aspects many times while trading. Perfect your technical knowledge and be cautious with them.

4. Take advantage of mock trading accounts. Using real accounts when starting options trading is a risky

game. You can lose a lot of cash within a short time duration. Mock accounts exist for a reason. You should test your trading skills in the mock accounts, learn a few tricks, and perfect your skills. The advantage of using a mock account is that there is no loss of money since they mostly provide virtual money. It prepares you for real trading. You should take advantage of them and learn a lot. Utilize them for a while and do some evaluations on your returns. When everything works out well, face real trading and shine.

5. Utilize limit orders. It is risky to rely on market prices since price behavior change with time. You should utilize limit orders when trading. A limit order is a type of order that enables you to purchase market securities at an agreed price. Using this type of order shuns you from incurring losses in options trading.

6. Revise your strategies with time. After entering into the options trading, with time, you need to revise your strategies. Utilize the working strategies more often and get rid of unsuccessful trading strategies. You should not have many strategies that do not bring good performance. Few working strategies are better than having multiple ones that do not help you.

7. Register and join in options trading platforms. Joining forums comprised of other options traders is another

way of how to get started in options trading. Forums are platforms of different people with different experiences and opinions. You can learn mistakes made by others in trading. It is part of growing in options trading. So why shouldn't you give it a try?

8. Study and learn about trading metrics. Having your returns maximized is also another way of getting started in options trading. Traders normally use different trading metrics such as delta, gamma, theta, and vega. You should learn and practice them for massive returns.

OPTIONS STRATEGIES

Strangles

One of the simplest strategies that go beyond simply buying options, hoping to profit on moves of the underlying share price, is called a strangle. This strategy involves buying a call option and a put option simultaneously. They will have the same expiration dates, but different strike prices. If the price of the stock rises the put option will expire worthless (but of course it may still hold a small amount of value when you closed your position, and you can sell it and recoup some of the loss). But you will make a profit off the call option. On the other hand, if the stock price declines, the call option will expire worthlessly, but you can make a profit from the put option.

In this case, you can make substantial profits no matter which way the stock moves, but the larger the move, the more profits. On the upside, the profit potential is theoretically unlimited. On the downside, the stock could theoretically fall to zero, so there is a limit, but potential gains are substantial.

The breakeven price on the upside is the strike price of the call plus the amount of the two premiums settled for the options.

If the stock price declines the break-even price would be the difference between the strike value of the put option and the sum of the two premiums paid for the options.

Straddles

When you purchase a call and a put option with similar strike amounts and expiration dates, this is called a straddle. The idea here is that the trader is hoping the share price will either rise or fall by a significant amount. It won't matter which way the price moves. Again, if the price rises the put option will expire worthless, if the price falls the call option will expire worthlessly. For example, suppose a stock is trading at $100 a share. We can buy at the money call and put options that expire in 30 days. The price of the call and put options would be $344 and $342 respectively, for a total investment of $686.

With 20 days left to expiration, suppose the share price rises to $107. Then the call is priced at $766, and the put is at $65. We can sell them both at this time, for $831 and take a profit of $145.

Suppose that, instead of at 20 days to expiration, the share price dropped to $92. In that case, the call is priced at $39, and the put is priced at $837. We can sell them for $876, making a profit of $190.

So, although the profits are modest compared to a situation where we had speculated correctly on the directional move of the stock and bought only calls or puts, this way we profit no matter which way the share price moves. The downside to this strategy is that the share price may not move in a big enough way to make profits possible. Remember that extrinsic value will be declining for both the call and the put options.

Selling covered calls against LEAPS and other LEAPS Strategies

A LEAP is a long-term option, that is an option that expires at a date that is two years in the future. They are regular options otherwise, but you can do some interesting things with LEAPS. Because the expiration date is so far away, they cost a lot more. Looking at Apple, call options with a $195 strike price that expires in two years are selling for $28.28 (for a total price of $2,828). While that seems expensive, consider that 100 shares of Apple would cost $19,422 at the time of writing.

If you buy in the money LEAPS, then you can use them to sell covered calls. This is an interesting strategy that lets you earn premium income without having actually to buy the shares of stock.

LEAPS can also be used for other investing strategies. For example, if Apple is trading at $194, we can buy a LEAP option for $3,479 with a strike price of $190 that expires in two years. If, at some point during that two-year period, the share price rose to $200 we could exercise the option and buy the shares at $190, saving $10 a share. Also, at the same time, we could have been selling covered calls against the LEAPS.

Buying Put Options as Insurance

A put option gives you the right to sell shares of stock at a certain price. Suppose that you wanted to ensure your investment in Apple stock, and you had purchased 100 shares at $191 a share, for a total investment of $19,000. You are worried that the share price is going to drop and so you could buy a put option as a kind of insurance. Looking ahead, you see a put option with a $190 strike price for $4.10. So, you spend $410 and buy the put option.

Should the price of Apple shares suddenly tumble you could exercise your right under the put option to dispose of your shares by selling at the strike price to minimize your losses. Suppose you wake up one morning and the share price has dropped to $170 for some reason. Had you not bought the option you could have tried to get rid of your shares now and take a loss of $21 a share. But, since you bought the put option, you can sell your shares for $190 a share. That is a $1 loss since you purchased the shares at $191. However, you also have to take into account the premium paid for the put options contract, which was $4.10. So, your total loss would be $5.10 a share, but that is still less than the loss of $21 a share that you would have suffered selling the shares on the market at the $170 price. When investors buy stock and a put at the same time, it is called a married put.

Spreads

Spreads involve buying and selling options simultaneously. This is a more complicated options strategy that is only used by advanced traders. You will have to get a high-level designation with your brokerage in order to use this type of strategy. We won't go into details because these methods are beyond the scope of junior options traders, but we will briefly mention some of the more popular methods so that you can have some awareness.

One of the interesting things about spreads is they can be used by level 3 traders to earn regular income from options. If you think the price of a stock is going to stay the same or rise, you sell a put credit spread. You sell a higher-priced option and buy a lower-priced option at the same time. The difference in option prices is your profit. There is a chance of loss if the price drops to the strike price of the puts (and you could get assigned if it goes below the strike price of the put option you sold). You can buy back the spread, in that case, to avoid getting assigned.

If you think that the price of a stock is going to drop you can sell to open a credit spread. In this case, you are hoping the price of the stock is going to stay the same or drop. You sell a call with a low strike price and buy a call with a high strike price (both out of the money). The difference in price is your profit, and losses are capped.

We can also consider more complicated spreads.

For example, you can use a diagonal spread with calls. This means you buy a call that has a shorter expiration date but a strike amount that is higher, and then you sell a call with a longer expiration date and a lower strike price. This is done in such a way that you earn more, from selling the call, than you spend on buying the call for a considerable strike amount, and so you get a net credit to your account.

Spreads can become quite complicated, and there are many different types of spreads. If a trader thinks that the price of a stock will only go up a small amount, they can do a bull call spread. Profit and loss are capped in this case. The two options would have the same expiration date.

If you sell a call with a lower strike price and simultaneously buy a call with a high strike price, this is called a bear call spread. You seek to profit if the underlying stock drops in price. This can also be done by using two put options. In that case, you buy a put option that has a higher strike and sell a put option with a lower strike price.

A bull spread involves attempting to profit when the price of the stock rises by a small amount. In this case, you can also use either two call options or two put options. You buy an option with a lower strike price while selling an option with a higher strike price.

Spreads can be combined in more complicated ways. An iron butterfly combines a bear call spread with a bear put spread. The purpose of doing this is to generate steady income while minimizing the risk of loss.

An iron condor uses a put spread, and a call spread together. There would be four options simultaneously, with the same expiration dates but different strike prices. It involves selling both sides (calls and puts).

Iron Condor

If you think the price of a stock is going to stay within a certain range, you can sell to open an iron condor. This type of strategy requires you to buy a call and sell a call (creating a call credit spread) and buy a put and sell a put (creating a put credit spread). Let's see how it is built in steps. All options in this strategy have the same expiration date.

First, you pick an out of the money call price, a bit above the current share price. You sell this call. Then you buy one with a strike that is a little bit higher. The net difference gives you a credit.

Now you pick an out of the money put option, that is below the current share price. Then you sell this put option. You buy an out of the money put option that has an even lower strike price. The difference here gives you another credit.

The maximum profit is the net credits. The maximum loss is given by (width of strike prices) – entry price. The broker will make you put up enough cash to cover the loss unless you have a margin account.

The narrower you make your strike prices the lower your maximum loss, but the higher the probability that you will experience a loss. The range is set by the two options you sell, you want the stock price to stay within those bounds.

The iron condor is a great strategy to use for monthly income. It can work especially well over short time frames, like a week, since that lessens the chance of the stock going outside the range. However, many traders use a month for their iron condors.

Iron Butterfly

An iron butterfly is another strategy to use if you think the stock price will stay within a certain range. It will use four options, like the iron condor, but there will be three different strike prices.

In this case, you will sell a put option and a call option with the same strike price. The strategy is to get as close to at the money as possible. We will call the strike priced used the central strike.

Then you set a differential price we will call x. Now you buy a put option with a strike price of (central strike − x), and you buy a call option with a strike price of (central strike + x).

Like an iron condor, the profit from an iron butterfly is fixed at the net credit when you sell to open. This is given by the sum of the premiums earned from selling the at the money call and put, minus the prices paid for the out of the money options.

The maximum loss is the strike price of the purchased call − strike price of the sold put − total premium.

UNDERSTANDING PASSIVE INCOME

Options are perfectly capable of providing you with passive income, but what is passive income really? People seem to think that passive income is easy money and in some ways it is. However, the term easy misleads most people to think that passive income doesn't involve any work. This is not the truth at all.

Understanding the nature of passive income will help you figure out a lot about how options trading works since it cuts right to the heart of successful options trading. So let's begin by defining and taking a look at passive income.

Passive Income

There are, broadly speaking, two ways of making money. The first is to exchange your time for money and the second is to exchange your money for money. The first way is to undertake something like a job or to freelance. You're investing your time into a project and in return you get paid. Yes, you're really getting paid for a result if you're freelancing but my point is that it takes time to produce that result.

The more time you spend on such tasks, the more your earning ability is. If you're a freelance writer, for example, the greater the number of high quality words you produce, the more you're going to get paid per month. Thus, one of the important things to note about this sort of income is that when you go to sleep, so does your income stream.

When asked about one of the key things that rich people do that poor people don't, Bill Gates responded by saying that the rich leverage their time a lot better (Bodnar, 2017). What does leveraging time mean? Well, Gates' point was that the only thing that is truly limited in our lives is time. We cannot get back the time we've lost, no matter how much we would like to believe that time machines exist.

So ultimately, being financially successful comes down to how well you manage your time. The fact of the matter is that a rich person manages to get paid more for a unit of their time than a poor person does. So how do you get paid more per hour?

Leveraging Time

One easy way is to upskill yourself. Simply learn a higher skill and work in a more lucrative field. However, even this doesn't fully leverage your time since once you go to sleep, your money tap is switched off. Hence, the thing to do is to create multiple streams of income. If you have two streams of income paying you at the same time, you can double your hourly wage.

The problem is that you can only do so much at once. You can't perform two jobs at the same moment of time. So what you really want is another source of income that doesn't place demands on your time which will detract you from your job or hourly source of money. This is precisely what a passive income stream is.

Passive streams leverage your time by simply providing you with an additional amount of money for no additional input of time. I want to make something clear at this point; you will need to spend time creating and maintaining the passive income stream. My point is that your earning ability with this stream doesn't directly depend on how many hours you put into it.

If you spend five hours writing, you're going to get paid for the words you produced in those five hours. If you spend five hours on a passive income stream, you're not going to necessarily get paid for those five hours. You could get paid less, you could get paid more, who knows? The point is that whatever comes, adds to your income as long as you spend the time to do things correctly.

For example, a savings account provides you with passive income. A real estate investment on which you earn rent provides you with passive income. You can spend ten hours a day maintaining your property or spend two hours, it doesn't matter. It will earn you the market level of rent as long as things are maintained properly. There is an aspect of marginal utility with passive income, as economists call it (Bloomenthal, 2019).

Marginal utility refers to the return you receive, in satisfaction or dollars, for every unit of work spent. So if you spend five hours fixing the taps, that is probably going to make you good money. Spending an additional hour figuring out which exact shade of white the walls need to be painted with is probably not going to make you much. Hence, the marginal utility of the former is a lot higher than the latter.

All passive income streams have a level of maximum marginal utility before the returns start dropping off. Trading options, if you're catching on, is subject to the same forces. Remember that your return is measured not just in money but also in the satisfaction and quality of life you receive. So you need to figure out this value first.

A good way of understanding the value you'll receive and checking which style of trading you wish to adopt is to understand the styles of trading themselves. This way, you can make an accurate judgment of what suits you best.

Active and Passive Trading

As far as the SEC is concerned, all trading is active. Passive actions are reserved for the investment world. Whatever the good folk of the SEC might think, in reality, there are active forms of trading as well as passive forms. The diversity of the markets means that there exist many ways in which you can divide trading activity. Active versus passive simply happens to be one method of doing so.

Active trading refers to what you think traders actually do. This is where people sit glued to their terminals waiting on tenterhooks for news items to be released and then acting like hotshots when they make money. All of this is accurate except for that last bit which is a caricature. Either way, active trading usually involves taking directional bets on the market and usually hedging that with some other financial instrument.

Institutional traders, the kinds that trade for hedge funds, big banks and proprietary trading firms (prop shops), are all active traders. No matter what sort of strategies they employ and no matter which instruments they trade, they're always in touch with the markets. They need to be this way because their objective is to squeeze every ounce of money available.

In order to do so, they have to follow the market's every move. They need to know the market backwards and cannot have things sneak up on them. What's more, they need to deal with unexpected things that happen over holidays or weekends. For example, as of this writing, oil traders around the world have had to deal with the repercussions of a couple of Saudi Arabian oil fields being attacked.

This happened over the weekend and when the markets were closed. As they returned to work on Monday, you can bet that none of them had slept through the weekend. Active traders tend to look at this sort of thing as an opportunity. Market mispricings happen during such events and opportunities present themselves. One needs to love the adrenaline rush that occurs during such times. It's no surprise then, that at big banks, the average trader spends about five years on a desk before moving onto a managerial position where they supervise other traders who ultimately place all the bets.

It just isn't easy keeping up with such a lifestyle, after all. In contrast to this active trader, we have the passive trader. The passive trader's returns are not comparable to the active one's. This doesn't mean they make less money, just that they make less than the average active trader.

The tradeoff is that they get to spend their time doing something else. Understandably, a lot of big banks look down upon this sort of thing since a good quality of life on the trading desk usually means losses. However, some hedge funds and other private institutions welcome this sort of thing actively.

You see, a holy grail in the financial world is the pursuit of market neutral returns. Market neutral means that the strategy makes money no matter what the market does. In such strategies, a trader sets things up via complex financial instruments and then lets the market play itself out. This doesn't mean they go to sleep after this, they simply recycle the strategy in as many markets as possible.

Thus, while the strategy is passive the trader is active by choice in such institutions. There are sole traders who fix their level of activity within prop shops by trading this way. There is a lot of freedom in such strategies since the trader is not chained to their desk out of necessity. They can vary their involvement in the market and while the returns don't compare to active strategies, the overall payoff is worth it to the trader.

Almost every passive strategy involves the use of options. The ones that don't involve the usage of derivatives that behave like options.

Pros and Cons of Passive Income

While there seem to be a lot of positives from passive income, I must warn you that it isn't all a bed of roses. Even roses have thorns, after all. The negatives that lend themselves to passive income almost entirely have to do with how people approach it. A lot of people think that this is lazy money and that things run on autopilot.

Well, this is not the case at all. Every passive income stream, including the ones to do with trading require investment of either time or money or both. In the case of passive trading income, you need to invest both. Time is needed to learn and study the markets and to develop your skills.

The markets are not easily deciphered mainly because they are chaotic. Our brains are designed to handle linear environments and understand step by step patterns easily. However, patterns that present themselves intermittently, rhyming with one another instead of replicating themselves exactly, are an alien language.

Thankfully, our brains are learning machines and over time, we can learn to spot such patterns. This is really what trading is all about. Time is needed to train your brain to get used to this new world where everything happens at random but plays out according to a perfectly predictable bigger picture.

Therefore, you need to spend time learning the markets and understanding the ins and outs of options. You need to learn their characteristics to such an extent that you should instantly be able to decide whether to adjust a trade or not. Options trades are complex on the surface since they involve at least two legs. Adjustment is a case of removing both legs or just one and establishing another leg elsewhere.

This calls for mental agility, so you need to spend time to work up to this level. Do not expect to be able to do this overnight. The other thing to invest into this is money. This is simple enough to understand. You need money to trade and as mentioned earlier, your level of capitalization is going to determine how long you can survive.

This sounds like a bleak thing to say but it's better to assume the worst in these situations in order to set yourself up for long term success. This way, there's no chance you'll ever take this endeavor lightly. Now that I've addressed the negatives, let's look at the positives.

Simply put, passive income can make you money while you sleep. It also frees up your time to do more things since you'll eventually reach a stage where your passive income exceeds your active income. This gives you the option to quit your job and do something else with your time. At this point, most people decide to set up another source of passive income which further leverages their time.

Done in this way, passive income brings the power of compounding into effect since one stream builds another and so on. What I mean is that let's say you set aside $30,000 for trading options, after a lot of preparation and practice. Let's assume you generate $15,000 on this money after taxes. After five years of such returns, assuming you reinvested all your cash, you'll have enough for a down payment for a house or a real estate deal.

If you invest your trading returns into a real estate deal and earn a good 100% return there, you can further take that money and put it elsewhere. Passive income simply gives you more options and the chain of returns all began with a much smaller initial investment. The thing about passive income is that it will look small initially but as the amounts pile up later, the power of compounding takes over and your returns will become huge.

Passive income is thus exponential in nature but you need to give it time to mature. Trading options is just one way of generating passive income but there are a lot of other ways of doing so. Within the options trading world, there are a number of strategies you can employ depending on your comfort level with them, as we'll shortly see.

Options prices are determined in part by the price of the underlying stock. But options prices are also influenced by the time left to expiration and some other factors. We are going to go over all the different ways that the price of a given option can change and what will be behind the changes. It's important to have a firm grasp of these concepts so that you don't go into options as a naïve beginning trader.

How Options Prices are Determined

Market price of shares

The largest factor that impacts the price of an option is the price of the investment known as the stock that is behind the option. However, it's not a 1-1 relationship. The amount of influence from the underlying stock is going to change with time. Furthermore, it depends on whether the option is in the money, at the money, or out of the money. The fraction of the options price that is due to the price of the underlying stock is called the options intrinsic value.

If an option can be exactly the same as the market pricing or not be comparatively favored, it has zero intrinsic value. An option would have to be priced in the money in order to have any intrinsic value.

- For a call option, if the market price is lower than the strike price or the same, the option will have no pricing at all from the intrinsic value. If the share price is higher than the price used to trade shares via the option, the option will have intrinsic value.

- For a put option, if the share price is at or above the strike price, the option will have zero intrinsic value. If the share price is below the strike price, then the option will have some value from the stock. This is called intrinsic value.

However, to confuse matters, even when an option is at or out of the money, the price of the underlying stock has some influence that can change the value of the option. The amount of influence that the market price of the item known as the stock has on the price of the option is given by a quantity that is called delta. You can read the value for delta by looking at the data for any option that you are interested in trading. It is given as a decimal value ranging from 0 to 1 for call options, and it's given as a negative value for put options. The reason it's given as a negative value for put options is that this reflects the fact that if the stock price is found to increase, the price of a put option will be reduced. In contrast, if the stock price declines, the value of the put option will increase. It's an inverse relationship, and thus, the delta is negative for put options.

To understand how this will play out, let's look at a specific example. Suppose that we have a $100 option. That is, the strike price is set to $100. If the price of the underlying stock is $105, delta for the call option is 0.77.

That means that if the dollar value of the stock increases by $1, the value of the option will rise by approximately 77 cents. This is a per-share price change. So, for the option that you are trading, there are 100 underlying shares. So, a 77 cent price rise would actually increase the value of the option by $77.

For a put option with the same strike price, the option would be out of the money, because the share price is higher than the strike price. In this case, for the put option, the delta is given as -0.23. That means that the put option would lose approximately $23 if the share price went up by $1. On the other hand, if the share price dropped by $1, the put option would gain $23.

The intrinsic value of the call option described in this theoretical exercise would be $5 per share. The total cost of the option would be $6.06 per share, reflecting the fact that the call option has $1.06 in extrinsic value. In contrast, the put option has zero intrinsic value. It has almost the same extrinsic value, however, at $1.03.

I have used a 45-day time frame prior to expiration for this exercise. Options prices are actually governed by mathematical formulas, so it's possible to make estimates of what the option price is going to be ahead of time. There are many calculators and spreadsheets that are available free online for this purpose.

Now, let's say that instead, the share price was $95 so that the call option was out of the money and the put option was in the money. In this case, the call option has zero intrinsic value, and it has a $0.94 extrinsic value, so the option would be worth $94. Delta has switched, but not exactly. In this case, for the call option, the delta is 0.25. If the share price rose to $96, with everything else unchanged, the price of the call option would rise to $1.21 per share. This illustrates that you can still earn profits from cheaper out of the money options.

Implied Volatility

One of the most important characteristics of options after considering delta and time decay is the amount a stock price varies with time. Volatility will give you an idea of how wild the price swings of stock are. If you look at a stock chart, I am sure that you are used to seeing the price go up and down a lot giving a largely jagged curve. The more that it fluctuates, and the bigger the fluctuations in price, the higher the volatility. Of course, everything is relative and so you can't say that any stock has an "absolute" level of volatility. What is done is the volatility for the entire market is calculated, and then the volatility of a stock is compared to the volatility of the market as a whole. When looking at the stocks themselves, this is given by a quantity called beta.

If the stock generally moves with the stock market at large, beta is positive. If beta is 1.0, that means that it has the same volatility as the entire market. That is a stock with average volatility.

If beta is less than 1.0, then the stock doesn't have much volatility. The amount below 1.0 tells you how much less volatile the stock is in comparison to the market as a whole. So, if the beta is given as 0.7, this means that the stock is 30% less volatile than the market average.

If beta is greater than 1.0, then the stock is more volatile than the average. If you see a stock with a beta of 1.42, that means the stock is 42% more volatile than the average for the market.

If beta is negative, that means the stock, on average, moves against the market. When the market goes up, it goes down and vice versa. Most stocks don't have a negative beta but they are not hard to find either.

Volatility is a dynamic quantity, so when you look it up, you are looking at a snapshot of the volatility at that given moment. Of course, under most circumstances, it's not likely to change very much over short time periods like a few weeks or a month. There are exceptions to this, including earnings season.

Implied volatility is a quantity that is given for options. Implied volatility is a measure of the coming volatility that the stock price is expected to see over the lifetime of the option (that is until the expiration date).

One of the things that make options valuable is the probability that the price of the stock will move in a direction that is favorable to the strike price. When an option goes in the money, or deeper in the money (that is the share price moves even higher relative to the strike price of a call, or lower relative to the strike price of a put), the value of the option can increase by a large margin.

If a stock is more volatile, there is more chance of this happening, since the price is going to be going through larger price swings. Therefore, the higher the implied volatility, the higher the price of the option.

In the following, we will consider a hypothetical situation to illustrate. This time, we will look at an option that would have a strike price that was set to a hundred dollars and a $100 share price, so the option is exactly at the money. Here are the prices that you would see for some different values of implied volatility:

- Implied volatility = 40%: Option price is $562.
- Implied volatility = 20%: Option price is $282
- Implied volatility = 10%: Option price is $142
- Implied volatility = 80%: Option price is $1,119

That is for a call option.

As you can see, implied volatility has quite a large influence on the price of an option. For this reason, professional options traders look at implied volatility just as much as they look to the comparison between the strike price and the market stock price. One way to make profits is to seek out options that have high implied volatility.

Each quarter, companies report their earnings. This is one time when implied volatility is going be really important. As mentioned earlier, earnings calls can send the price of a stock up or down by a large amount. Prices can move $10, $20, or $40 a share in one direction or the other depending on whether the earnings call beat expectations or not, and whether or not there was a piece of good or bad news thrown in with the earnings report. In other words, this is a highly volatile situation.

This offers opportunities for profits. The way that professional traders handle this is they purchase options on companies that are going to have upcoming earnings calls. Typically, you might purchase options about a week ahead of the earnings call. At that time, the implied volatility is going to be relatively low. It may be in the range of 15-20%.

As time passes and it gets closer to the earnings call, implied volatility will go up by a lot. In fact, for the examples above it was no accident that I selected implied volatility of 80%. Recently, I noticed that the implied volatility on some Tesla options shot up to 82%. As the implied volatility goes up, the value of the option increases, providing an opportunity for profits.

Time Decay

If an option is valued so that it is the same as the share price, or if it is out of the money, time decay is going to have a significant influence over the value of an option at any given time. For an option that can be said to be in the money, the influence of time decay is going to be much less. The closer you get to the expiration date, time value exerts less influence on the overall price of the option. In that case, it's going to be more influenced by implied volatility and the underlying share price. To take an example, at four days to expiration, a $100 strike price on an underlying stock when the market price is set equal to $110 per share will have $10 in intrinsic value with $0.56 in extrinsic value and a total price per share of $10.56. So the price is heavily weighted to the underlying price of the shares. However, theta is -0.23, meaning that on a per-share basis, at market open the following day, the option will lose $0.23 in value, all other things being equal. Of course, all other things are not equal, and changes in share price and implied volatility may wipe that out or add to it.

The important thing to do is check theta every afternoon so you can estimate what the cost is going to be for holding the option overnight. Time decay is an exponential phenomenon, so it decays faster the closer you get to the expiration date. The important path for the trader is knowing when other factors are going to be more important than time decay, you are not simply going to sell off your option because it's going to lose value from time decay the following morning.

Risk-Free Rate

You are also going to see the risk free rate quoted for an option. This is the interest rate that you could earn on an ideal safe investment. Generally speaking, this would be the interest you could earn from a 10-year U.S. treasury over the time period of the option. In normal times, this is an important factor to consider. Rising interest rates (that is significantly rising) can lower the value of options. In recent years, interest rates have been very low, and changes in interest rates have been small and very conservative. So at the present time at least, this is not really something to worry about.

Summary: The Greeks

The Greeks tell us the sensitivity to changes in the factors behind the contract that impact the price of the option.

- Delta: This measures how much the price of the option will vary if there is a single dollar move in the share price, and it also gives the probability that the option contract will come to an end favorably for the buyer. That is it would be in the money.
- Theta: This tells you the amount the price would decline by if a single day has passed. Its impact is felt when the market opens.

- Vega: This measures how responsive the option is if there is an alteration in implied volatility. It tells you how much the price of the option will change in response to a 1% change in the implied volatility.

- Rho: This tells you how responsive the option is to a variation of the risk-free interest rate. It estimates how much the price of the option will change in response to a 1% change in interest rates.

- Gamma: This tells you how much delta will be varying as a result of a change in the underlying stock price.

Before you invest in an option, you should check the values of the greeks. Then determine the relationship of the option strike price. Ask if it is in the money or out of the money, and determine what the implied volatility is.

Volume and Open Interest

Volume and open interest are not going to be factors you consider when trading an option. However, you also need to consider how difficult it's going to be when exiting a position. If you buy an option, you want to be able to sell it quickly in order to take profits at a level that you're comfortable with.

Some options might look appealing on the surface, but if you can't buy and sell them quickly, they might be more trouble than they are worth. So, you want the trading activity to be taking place at a reasonable level.

Open interest will tell you the number of option contracts that are out there on the market. This is for a single strike price. It would also be for the same expiration date and one type of option. So, if I have a Tesla call option, consider the possibilities. Suppose that there is a strike price of $250 that expires on August 2, I can look at the open interest to see how many of these contracts are on the market. Generally speaking, you want the open interest to be 100 or higher. For some highly traded securities, the open interest can be in the thousands. This is a dynamic quantity, it will change if more traders sell to open. But the rule of thumb is that 100 or higher gives you enough action on that contract that you can buy or sell later without having to wait a terribly long time to close the position. If open interest is really low, you might not find a buyer or seller at all.

Volume is a measure of how many times that option was traded on the current (if the markets are open) or previous trading days.

Conclusion

Bearing in mind that an option is all about the right to buy a stock, it might seem strange that most traders are not looking to do that. Instead, they are looking to immediately pass the stock on as a sell, making the profit by taking the premium along with the increased price on the stock from what they paid for it.

That's what you should be basing your strategy around: the idea of gaining stocks to instantly sell back onto the options market, making your profit in the process. In 99 out of 100 cases, that's what you will be aiming to do.

Nevertheless, there are still going to be times when you want to exercise your right in order to purchase the underlying stock itself. Usually, this is when you genuinely want to add a particular stock to your portfolio. It's up to you to decide when those times arrive.

First things first: be very aware that you will automatically exercise your right at the expiration date if the option is in the money unless you tell your broker not to take that action. That won't happen if it's out of the money, but it's still imperative that you keep a calendar of your trades so that you aren't surprised by the sudden arrival of stocks in your portfolio you'd completely forgotten about.

If and when you decide to exercise your right, you should almost always do it at the expiration date and not before, because you'll lose the time value if you exercise early. When you alert your broker to this decision, it's also important to know that you cannot then change your mind – the decision is permanent.

Buying puts can be a winning strategy if done right. The stock market wouldn't be the stock market if it only moved in one direction; by buying puts as well as calls, you're making the most of the market by profiting no matter which direction it's heading. Puts, during a bear market, are your ally.

Buying a put means that you are going to make a profit through the stock declining in price. Just as you're looking for the stock to skyrocket in a call, you're looking for it to plunge in a put. The strategy is therefore very similar, it's just that you're looking in the opposite direction.

Most traders buy puts either because they're speculating on a stock and think they can make a profit in a short term as that stock plummets, or because they can function as insurance for your overall portfolio. If you actually own the stock in question, you can buy puts on it if you believe it's at risk of heading downwards.

For instance, let's say you own stocks in a company and you think the business environment is going to see the share price drop. You aren't sure, but you can make an educated guess. Simply leaving that stock sitting in your portfolio means potentially watching as its value bleeds away.

On the other hand, you could buy a put and give yourself the option to offload that stock if it does drop to a certain value. As the buyer, you are not obligated to sell your stock when the deadline arrives – you're just giving yourself the option to do so. Of course, as always, you'll lose the premium.

The biggest difference between buying calls and puts is that the stock market has a habit of falling much faster than it rises. A stock can drop through the floor in just a single day, whereas it can take weeks or months to climb to magical figures.

To buy puts for the sake of speculation, you'll need to master the art of spotting weaker stocks – the ones that are likely to fall. This is easiest during a bear market and when the overall economic outlook is poor.

Even the most successful companies have down times, after all, and if you own a put contract when that happens, you stand to make money.

When buying a put, you'll need to think in reverse. The lower the strike price, the cheaper the option will be (in other words, the opposite of buying a call). You should also factor in the speed of the market when looking at expiration dates. If you think the stock is going to drop hard and fast, you probably want a shorter deadline. If you think it will take a while for the full effects of the drop to realize, then you will want a longer one.

The most successful put strategies, at least at first, will probably be slightly in the money, because you can profit from a smaller change in the underlying value. Conversely, you'll make more money on a smaller premium with an out of the money put, but you have less chance of actually making that money.

Selling puts can be a gamble. The idea behind it is that, by selling your promise to buy stocks, you are earning a steady premium, but you're choosing contracts that you believe will never hit the strike price. That way, you walk away having been paid for the contract without having to actually own the underlying stock.

It's also a way to increase your stock portfolio and get paid for doing so. This can be useful if you think a stock's dropping price is temporary and you want to snap up a few of them before they start to rise again, when you can sell them on.

Be aware, of course, that when selling a put you are obligating yourself to buy that stock if it does reach the strike price, so it's a bad gamble if you lack the funds to do that when the deadline comes.

www.ingramcontent.com/pod-product-compliance
Lightning Source LLC
Chambersburg PA
CBHW071407210526
45465CB00001B/287